THE YEAR THAT
CHANGED MY MIND!

Kay Jane

1976 -The Year that Changed My Mind By Kay Jane

ISBN: 978-0-578-77751-1

Scripture quotations are taken from
the King James Version of the Bible.

Content

Endorsement for
1976 -The Year that Changed My Mind
By Kay Jane

Kay Jane candidly explores the depths of her questions around issues of abortion. This captivating story winds around her most transitional coming-of-age year, 1976. Cultural and historical clashes become a metaphorical backdrop for Kay Jane's inward struggles.

Readers will benefit from Kay Jane's sensitivity and expression clarifying for her, and hopefully others, this important issue that still draws controversy for many Americans today. Once I started reading her book, I couldn't put it down!

- *Maude Wells*

Introduction

Life is a gift we all need to treasure with the choices we make. The twelve month journey of the events that were happening in the country and world are part of the narrative.

The names have been changed to protect the identity of the individuals whose life experiences have been shared. There are a few events that were moved to this year from the previous year for the purpose of telling the story.

There are many things that shape and mold us into who we are. This is a brief glimpse as history is shared and how it influences our opinions and ideas. You can allow culture to unravel you only to find out that the truth has the ability to set you free. May you find something that resonates with your experiences or just appreciate someone's year of awakening.

Some people regard discipline as a chore. For me, it is a kind of order that sets me free to fly.

- Julie Andrews

CHAPTER 1

JANUARY - THE YEAR BEGINS

The year is 1976 and our country is celebrating its 200th year of Independence. I live with my parents, two bothers Joe and Stan, and our dog Chip, in Pennsylvania. Pennsylvania is known as the Keystone state for the pivotal role in seeing the United States established as a nation. My home sits next to our family business where employees and my family work hard to provide quality plants and flowers to our community and the surrounding areas. Living in the land of freedom allows people to invest their lives into establishing businesses.

Freedom was not something I thought too much about before a history class I had in a seventh grade public school. In this class we worked on contracts with questions that we had to answer and activities to do by ourselves. We did research in the library, wrote short essays, or watched a super eight film loop. One particular contract that I worked on was the History of World War II. One part of this contract was to watch a film on the liberation of a concentration camp. At this point in my life, I was unaware what happened in these camps.

I popped the film in the player and closed the door and turned off the light. I was in a dark utility room and I sat down to flip the switch on the player. The film started and to my horror the events that transpired before my eyes were shocking and terrifying. I saw human suffering beyond what I had ever seen.

There were images of people so emaciated you could see almost every bone in their bodies. Piles of dead bodies were lying on top of each other; these scenes were so sickening. There was no one to talk to about this afterwards and it was hard to process what I had just seen. These horrific deeds were done at the hand of other humans. The only thing that seemed to console me was the fact that this happened over thirty years ago.

My grandmother would often calm my fears as she shared her wisdom and insights on life. She was big on appreciating what you have and being thankful. She was also an advocate for the Native Americans and the many injustices that they had experienced. My cousin thought she might be a Native American because of her high cheekbones and dark complexion. I believe her heart was tender towards them from all they had suffered.

Just as the Native Americans enjoyed the seasons and the beauty each season holds, my grandmother recognized our state for it's loveliness. The winter with the snow and ice crystals, spring with abundant greens and full array of blooms, summer with the gardens bounty and fresh flavors, and fall with the myriad of colorful leaves ornamenting the landscape. I had to agree with her, when I would travel to other areas of the country I felt like Dorothy from The Wizard of Oz: click my heels and say, "There's no place like home".

It was now winter and this would be my final year of high school as I had made plans to skip my junior year. One of the reasons for making this decision was not being part of any particular group. In grade school I was the only girl in the slow reading group and was shunned by my classmates. This can be hard for a young child and although I was eventually perceived differently, as I got older it left a lasting imprint of insecurity and rejection.

My parents said I would have to plan what I would do after high school. The only class that I would have to drop in order to graduate a year early was an aviation class in order to take an extra English class. I loved that aviation class but knew I would not follow through with the expensive lessons on learning how to fly. The confidence I had gained in this class with a wonderful teacher was well worth my time.

I had learned how an airplane worked in this class, like the wings with the ailerons, flaps, the tail with the elevators, and rudder. There are VFR (Visual Flight Rules) pilots, those who can fly when the visibility is good and IFR (Instrument Flight Rules) pilots who can fly a plane by the instruments with no need for a visual of the landscape. At the end of the first semester a local pilot took us up in a Helio Courier, which could take off in a short distance. The engines were geared up for take-off and were pretty loud. You could not hear the person next to you.

The plane began to move down the field and we were up in the air in short order. As we ascended we went through the treetops and soon we could look down at the landscape and see the fields, creeks, and farms that dotted the landscape. It was a truly exhilarating experience to be like a bird for a moment in time just soaring over such a beautiful scene. This new adventure was soon to come to an end as we landed in a short area in the field.

That is why this particular plane was used during the Vietnam War to carry a portable address system to broadcast appeals to the Vietcong. The Vietnam War was in the headlines for years and President Nixon talked of the war ending and bringing the troops home. The country was very divided by this war and a lot of protesting was happening on college campuses.

President Richard Nixon had won the election in 1972 and Spiro Agnew was the Vice President. Spiro Agnew resigned from the office of Vice President in 1973 because of kickbacks he had received when he was Governor of Maryland. Gerald Ford was appointed to the position of vice president in 1973. In the wake of the Watergate investigations, Richard Nixon resigned as president in 1974 and the vice president, Gerald Ford, became president of the United States of America. We had an unelected president in office for the 1976 election year.

There was another issue happening that did not garner the same press as the war and the resignation of a president. It was Roe v. Wade. The name Jane Roe represented a woman who sought to have an abortion, but the law of the state of Texas banned abortions. The case was taken to the U.S. Supreme Court which overrode the Texas law banning abortion, effectively legalizing abortion across the United States on January 22, 1973.

I liked to think of myself as a liberated woman and that a woman had a right to take charge of her body. Gloria Steinem was a journalist and spokeswoman for the American feminist movement at the time. Many women had been talking about the oppression of women through job discrimination, doing the same job as a man for less pay. Women were being exploited for just being a woman, and not talented individuals they were adding to the culture, business, and the corporate world.

We were given the right to vote in 1919, but who was representing us? So the 1973 ruling for women to have the right to an abortion seemed like a logical progression for women to be able to command their own future.

The future was being considered by other classmates as well as they had decided to graduate this year too. One of my classmates found out she was pregnant and decided to marry the father of the child. The baby was due in the summer and she would be able to graduate at the end of this school year. The other students had jobs, trade schools, or colleges they wanted to attend. As a whole we were a group of individuals that did not participate in many extracurricular activities. Where else in life would you be surrounded by so many peers that are your age? School was for learning, but it was not like the world we were about to enter once we graduated.

I had wanted to be an advertising artist, but my high school art teacher said I was not talented enough to pursue a career in that field. This comment was heartbreaking because being creative was a great passion of mine. My father thought I should spend more time doing schoolwork and stop wasting my time drawing. A new career path would need to be charted with realistic goals.

I made an appointment to see the guidance counselor. Her office was located in the main hallway in the front entrance to the school. When I visited Miss Harper's office she was very encouraging in helping me examine my options. She had a list of possibilities for me to choose from. One of the careers that sparked some interest was Occupational Therapy. This profession helped people of all ages learn to do everyday skills after an injury or illness.

Miss Harper helped me with the next step in the process. She found a list of colleges offering Occupational Therapy programs. I opted to look at places that had a two year Occupational Therapy Assistant program. I did not consider myself very studious and a two-year program would be more manageable for me. This educational path would leave the possibility of eventually doing two more years of school to become an Occupational Therapist, if all went well.

She found a school that was still accepting applications for the fall semester. She also helped make an appointment to visit the school and see what they had to offer. I had to complete the classes at hand and give this last semester of high school my best. To be successful would require some effort on my part as hope was arising with each new step.

The new semester had begun and the extra English class I had to take to graduate focused on composition and a review of grammar. Miss Carlton had been a student teacher in an English class I had the previous year. She was hired by our school district to be a full time teacher after she graduated from college. Her job was to teach us the things we had not learned, or had forgotten over the past couple of years.

As a new teacher she had enthusiasm that was contagious. We started with the simple task of diagramming sentences. This concept of learning the parts of speech seemed to elude me over the years as it seemed so abstract. She saw I was struggling and offered to break down each part to the simplest of terms so I could finally understand something that had been so foreign to me before.

Since Miss Carlton had been helping me, I asked her how I could prepare for the SAT's? She supplied me with vocabulary enrichment books that gave an unusual word and several meanings to choose from. She said, "this would comprise part of the test". She also provided me with reading comprehension material. You would read the story and a series of tricky questions followed. Thorough reading was necessary to get the right answer. She was a great help to me.

Another person who was an encouragement to me while making some hard decisions was my boyfriend Dean. While in third grade our class played the flute-o-phones for the spring concert. Dean sang a solo that evening from the musical *The Sound of Music*; the song, "Edelweiss". The s'es would whistle through the retainer he wore to correct an overbite. His talent, charm, and appearance had a great impact on me. There was a tenderness that reverberated as he sang for the audience. Hearing him sing that song made a lasting impression on me.

Dean was a friend of my brothers before he was my boyfriend. He had been around our house for years. One time when he came to see my brother, I remember my mom giving me the eyes. You know the one where you smile and raise your eyebrows like, "boy he's cute"!

Early one morning, while I was waiting for the bus, Dean drove by and flipped his lights on his car. He could make them go up and then disappear into the hood of his car. It was a bright red 1973 Opel GT. From then on, I would wave as he would drive by every morning on his way home from work. He always had a big smile on his face as he drove by.

The big yellow school bus was my mode of transportation to school everyday. My classmates thought this was ridiculous since I had access to a car, so why didn't I drive? My parents thought the bus was just fine since it was provided for transportation to school and I was all right with following their logic. I would catch a bus that stopped about two blocks away on the Main Street of my town.

One day, when I was waiting for the bus, Dean stopped and offered me a ride to school. He had a few brothers in school and I assumed he needed to take something to school for them, so I said, "Yes". Little did I know what was coming. He wanted to know if I wanted to go see Frank Zappa in concert at the Spectrum in Philadelphia. Somehow my mind went blank. What I originally thought this moment was, turned into something I had only dreamed of. I said, "yes"! The euphoria I felt for the rest of the day was like floating on clouds.

We went to the Frank Zappa concert and it was pretty exciting. He was one of those musical artists that thrived on shocking his audience. His music was fun, creative, and you were taken on a musical journey. All the musicians in his band were top-notch as he highlighted each one in a solo of songs that were performed throughout the evening. After the concert was over it took a while to maneuver through the seats and crowds. We headed home and I fell asleep as we got on the turnpike for the long ride home. It was a great concert and I found myself singing or humming some of the songs for the next few days.

Dean and I had been seeing each other for about two weeks when I told my mom I was going to marry him. The look she gave me was one of horror as you could imagine a mother responding to her sixteen-year-old daughter talking about marriage. She was left speechless. He was fun to be with and had some great skills as a magician. His sleight of hand in making things disappear was phenomenal.

At sixteen you can drive a car and make plans for the future, but there are no guarantees on how it will all turn out. It can be perplexing knowing which path to follow. I considered myself pro-choice on the abortion issue because the Supreme Court had made it legal. This law was relatively new and I was about to find out how close to home this decision would play out in our personal lives.

There was a new road trip on the horizon and it would prove to be a fun adventure. My older brother Joe and I went to pick up my younger brother, Stan, at college. Stan had gone there to study music in hopes of becoming a studio musician. Before he went, he spent hours practicing every day for many years. He had just made the decision to leave this school and work in the family business. We were all surprised that he would not be pursuing a career in music, but we loved and supported his choice to move on with his other interests. Planning for and developing who you are and what you want to become is not easy.

We had a seven hour drive ahead of us and decided to leave early to avoid any delays in New York City. The drive was filled with amazing mountain scenes and the beautiful industrial building scapes of the cities. I had never been to this city before, the home of the Boston Tea Party. It seemed fitting that we would come here on the anniversary of our nation. We got to experience some of this history with all the lovely cobblestone streets and fun local eateries. We even had a crash course on how to speak in a true city-style accent from a local who was more than willing to teach us.

I had heard that Rene, a friend of mine, was up here visiting her boyfriend. He was attending the same school as my brother and he was a musician too. I did not go out of my way to try to find her, but we were walking down a hallway and I happened to glance into a room to my left and saw her standing there with her boyfriend. I said, "Hey how are you?" She gave a simple wave and we moved on. I was a little disappointed that we did not have time to chat, but I was just happy and surprised to have seen her. I would let my classmates at the lunch table know I saw her when I got back to school on Monday.

"Whoever is happy will
make others happy."

- Anne Frank, The Diary of a Young Girl

CHAPTER 2
FEBRUARY - HAPPENINGS

When I went back to school the following week, I told my lunch table friends about seeing Rene with her boyfriend at the college. Shelly said, "You know why she was there don't you"? I told her, "I have no clue other than the fact that she was visiting her boyfriend." She then said, "She went there to have an abortion." Why did this hit me like a fist in the gut? All of a sudden the legalization of abortion became very personal to my world. Wow, I guess sixteen was pretty young to take on the responsibility of a baby. My mind was abuzz with, yes it is her choice, her body, but the reality and finality of that decision was so overwhelming to me at the time.

I sat at the table with these five friends for lunch for the last three years. They were a group of driven young ladies, working hard to prepare for a promising future. Sandra in particular was encouraged to become a doctor, but she wanted to be a nurse. Amy was great at mathematics and was going to pursue a career as a Public Accountant. They were all planning and fully engaged in the process of learning what they needed to know. They were committed to their studies and preparing for college.

Unlike this group who had such a clear vision of the future, some of us were unclear and put forth minimal effort. At first, I could not believe that Rene had made the decision to have an abortion, but then in my mind I tried to justify her choice in the realization of the responsibility. When she came back to school we all acted as if nothing had ever happened and nothing was said. She blended back into life with the same joy and enthusiasm she always lived. It's funny how in the back of your mind you're wondering if she's okay. You're afraid to ask because the answer may be beyond what you could comprehend.

I was making plans to move forward and visit the college that offered the Occupational Therapy program. At this point it was the only college that would even consider meeting with me, but I was optimistic that it would all work out. Kyle was a classmate who did well in school. He said he would study each subject every day to understand the material. His logic for learning would become a path for my personal change. Taking a calculated account of the information presented and ingesting what was taught.

One class that I had to work hard at was a speech class. So many of my classmates were so adept at public speaking. This class was smaller and a little more intimate. The teacher, Mrs. Pepper, had been my father's English teacher many years ago. I believe by the time she became my teacher her rules had relaxed considerably. I remember him sharing how she was a tough teacher when he had her for English.

Many would freely voice their opinions and insights in this class. My first speech was on explaining how to do something; and that was on how to de-bud a chrysanthemum. Growing up around various plants had given me some experiences others would not have had. Did you ever wonder how a mum plant had a single bloom on each stem?

My fear of speaking in public was paralyzing. I made a poster as a prop hoping I could concentrate on the poster instead of the students before me. The poster showed how each bud on the stem was taken off and the top bud was left to create the one beautiful flower on each stem. I was going along talking in a robotic fashion until my tongue was shaking so much I couldn't speak. Mrs. Pepper said, "Continue on, honey, you're doing great." All I could reply was, "I can't my tongue is shaking." With the help of the poster, I was able to follow the steps and systematically work my way through the remainder of the speech.

My next speech was about classical music, "The Brandenburg Concertos" by Johann Sebastian Bach was the piece of music I shared. There were no posters with this speech, just a record player with an album playing one of my favorites. I shared how classical music was so complex when compared to the music we would hear on the radio. I enjoyed rock music too, but also enjoyed the likes of Bach, Beethoven, and Vivaldi. This speech was timed and I was playing the music for a portion of my speech.

The uproar from my fellow classmates was surprising. They said that the time I used to play the music should be deducted from the time of the speech since I was not speaking. I was a little embarrassed and could see the reasoning behind their critique. I was surprised when the teacher came to my defense and said the music was a necessary part of my presentation. Well, this solicited the response of being the teacher's pet. However, I greatly appreciated my teacher being my champion.

Music was a big part of my life. Folk music like James Taylor and Seatrain, both told amazing stories through their music. But the two master storytellers were Jim Croce, "Time in a Bottle" and Harry Chapin, "Cat's in the Cradle". Joni Mitchell also had some amazing music with some thought-provoking lyrics in dealing with relationships and the world around us.

One of my favorites was Doc Watson, a more traditional bluegrass musician who used a flat-picking style on the acoustic guitar, which was so classically beautiful. Papa John Creach was a talented blues violinist who had played with other bands and could create music in any style. He was such a versatile artist.

One band, Kansas, was a combination of rock and classical style, which included a violin. The first album was named after the group Kansas and one of the songs on that album was, "Can I Tell You". The lyrics were stirring you to examine whether you believed in freedom and prove that you deserved it. The second album was Song of America and the lyrics were written by Kerry Livgren for the title song. The song seemed very patriotic and made you think about the past to consider the future of what it meant to be free.

The theme song for the Winter Olympics was Je t'aime and the events were happening in Innsbruck, Austria. The Winter Olympics were something I looked forward to watching every four years. My favorite event to watch was figure skating. As a young girl, my neighbor's grandfather made a rectangular frame out of wood in the freezing part of winter, covered the frame with plastic and filled it with water. When the water froze we would put our ice skates on and soar across the ice. We would pretend to be figure skaters as we spun in circles or did daring jumps.

This year Dorothy Hamill was the one to beat in the women's competition. In the men's category, Terry Kubicka did a backflip in his routine that was truly amazing. The ski jump and luge athletes traveled at high speeds and the accuracy they needed was a matter of life and death. Some of these events had you sitting on the edge of your seat as they sped down the hills.

Watching the television was a big part of what my mother and I did together. She was busy with her business from morning to night and watching an evening lineup of shows was her way of relaxing after a busy day. During supper my dad would turn on the evening news to find out what was happening locally as well as around the world.

My parents had traveled to many places around the globe. They went to Europe, England, Mexico, and Canada with an opportunity to experience other cultures. My dad was a Republican and my mom was a Democrat, so it made for some interesting discussions at the dinner table. I will call this dinner table politics, because a lot of what we take in is not taught, but caught in moments like these. It appears that you are just casually listening, but you are formulating thoughts and opinions on what is being said.

After supper we cleaned up the kitchen and got ready for bed. The night of programs would feature shows like *Happy Days*, a comedy show set in the 1950's and the antics of teenagers, *Little House on the Prairie,* which was loosely based on a book series written by Laura Ingalls Wilder. Another show was *Barney Miller*, a sitcom about a police department in New York City. Depending on the storyline, we would sometimes laugh or cry together. *MASH*, a comedy-drama was about a medical unit during the Korean War.

My church was pacifist in their beliefs, meaning they thought that war and violence were without merit. This teaching was brought home while attending a church camp years before and some of our camp counselors were conscientious objectors; they were assigned to civilian service instead of going into the military. They would strum their guitars and sing folk songs that had been written about the futility of war.

This made a big impression on me and how some took such a powerful stance on issues. Some of these conscientious objectors even left the country and went to Canada in order to avoid the mandatory draft. As a young person, I embraced this non-violent stance. In my simplistic thinking, if the men fighting out on the battlefield could sit down and talk to each other, would there be the possibility of a true friendship? Whose battle were they fighting anyway? I am no seasoned analyst, just a young person trying to make sense out of war.

My next battle was marked by a three and a half hour trip across the state to visit the college. This drive would be the longest I ever took by myself. A map was carefully laid out to help me determine which route was best. One way in particular was easy to follow, but it would be a little longer. I chose this route since it was my first cross state trip. The appointment was for 10 a.m. and I would leave at 6 a.m. to give myself a little time in case I got lost.

I woke up, got dressed and mixed up a strawberry flavored milkshake called Instant Breakfast. I had been using my brother Joe's 1972 Silver Cuda, with a vinyl black top as my mode of transportation. The car's gas tank had been filled the night before so I could concentrate on my journey to the northeastern part of the state. I grabbed my purse and said goodbye to my mom and was off on an adventure.

The scenery was gorgeous with lots of rolling hills and bare trees. One of the ways of getting through the mountains were long tunnels, tunnels where you cannot see the other end when you enter. The lights on the ceilings and the walls provided illumination, along with the headlights from the car imparting the light for the road ahead. The further I traveled, the higher the mountains became. Going through a nearby city, I started to ascend up one particularly huge incline. Snow dotted the ground the higher I went. At the top I would find my destination. There were capacious old distinguished buildings on a beautifully landscaped property.

Slowly, I turned into the parking lot to get my bearings as to where I should be. There was a red brick building to my right and it looked like that might be the place I wanted to be. I opened my door and took a deep breath as I headed to the main entrance. As I entered a young lady behind the counter greeted me with a smile and asked, "Do you have an appointment?" I said, "I do." She asked "What is your name?" I told her and she looked over her list. She said, "take a seat and someone will be with you shortly".

It wasn't long until a woman wearing a nun's habit came and introduced herself to me. "Hello, I'm Sister Clover and at this time acting dean of this college". My school counselor had told me it was a Catholic college, but honestly I was not sure what to expect. She was a very jolly individual which made any anxiety I was experiencing dissipate.

We went over my school records which were not impressive and she made me aware of the fact that I had some work to do. I would need a certain score on my SATs in order to be admitted to the college. So it was not a 'yes' at this time and she gave me something to work towards in the months ahead. It seemed so unsettling not having a definite answer. She assured me that it was doable and I sensed that she was going out on a limb to give me that glimmer of hope.

One of the students on campus was given the job of helping me get acquainted with the campus by giving me a tour of this quaint, beautiful place. The campus had a group of several old three-story brick buildings with ivy climbing up the sides. There was a lovely cathedral structure nestled at the back of one of the buildings down a lengthy walkway.

We went to see the dorms and my guide showed me the lounge with a few sofas, where the laundry was, and a vending machine to get snacks. She knocked on a door and asked those in residence if we could take a glance at their room. They opened the door to give us a peek and I was surprised at how neat the room was with this impromptu visit. We thanked them and moved on to the final building.

This was a rather new structure with large windows. As we walked in, it became apparent that it was the dining room with a lovely view into the woods. There were large pine and deciduous trees embellishing the landscape of the college that seemed to be pristinely situated on the side of the mountain. I thanked my tour guide for her time and we parted ways. I left wondering if this would become my future home.

"The pain I feel now is the happiness
I had before. That's the deal."

- C.S. Lewis

CHAPTER 3
MARCH - PLAYING THE FOOL

The ride on the school bus one particular morning was not pleasant at all. A young man on the bus decided to hit me on the top of the head with his knuckles. It came out of nowhere and was so unexpected and painful. I tried to be tough and not cry but it hurt so much. My eyes welled up with tears and a throbbing headache came on pretty quickly. He started laughing maniacally and I tried to ignore him, because I hate confrontation.

When I got to school I went to the bathroom to wash my face before heading to my morning classes. This random act of senseless violence would not be the only surprise to this day. The first few hours of the day were a blur and not much learning had occurred. Lunchtime would be the break my throbbing head needed.

My friend Sally stopped me right in front of the smoking bathrooms as I was passing by. The smoke was billowing out from beneath the door with its pungent and acrid odor. "Hey", she said, "I heard you have a boyfriend." I gave her a nod to the affirmative. She went on to tell me that she had gotten pregnant at a bad time in a relationship with her boy friend and had decided to have an abortion. She wanted to let me know if I ever needed her help she could point me in the right direction and what to do if I ever needed an abortion.

It seemed kind of odd that someone would just randomly stop you in the hall to share that bit of personal information. We were friends and I knew she cared about me. Yes, I believed it was a woman's right to determine what went on with her body. But I found it disquieting that Sally felt a need to make me aware of the information she had that could help me. I did not have that kind of relationship with my boyfriend. In a way it was a little unnerving as to why she had this impromptu need to share this information.

It seemed like it was one thing after another. Gym class came right after lunch. We all got changed into our shorts and t-shirts, and headed to the gym. As we all were waiting for instruction from our teacher, one of the girls started randomly singing "Happy Birthday" to me. All the other girls started to sing along with her, but it wasn't my birthday. I was unsure why I was chosen as her target, or was I overreacting to a harmless prank?

A few days later there was a drug raid at our school where dogs were brought in to sniff check our lockers. We were all directed out of the building while the search was made. For some reason I put my purse in my unlocked locker, trusting it would be safe there. The search continued while we stood outside. It was a sunny day with a brisk breeze as we waited for the all clear to return to our classes.

It was about a half hour until we were summoned back into the building. I made a quick stop at my locker and the purse was gone. That was a bit unnerving, not that it had a lot of money in it, just lunch money for the week. However, there were some senior pictures of friends who had already graduated in the little plastic photo pages in my wallet that I would be unable to replace.

Two weeks later my lunch group saw someone with my purse. They knew it was mine because the strap had ripped and I just tied the two ends in a knot to keep it together. Hating confrontations, my classmates took it upon themselves to approach the person with my purse and asked her, "Where did you get that purse?" She said she had just purchased it. They told her that the purse was mine and they knew she had stolen it. They were pretty riled up and wanted me to do something about it. The process for justice in this situation did not seem feasible. It was easier just to let it go and move on. As much as I liked the purse, just knowing someone else had used it as their own made it extremely undesirable to me.

The next morning we headed to our homerooms before we went to our first class. The girl sitting next to me felt it was her obligation to point out one of my features; my nose in particular, and let me know she thought it was rather large in proportion to my face. This was a very strange and uncomfortable situation as she stared at me in silence waiting for me to answer. I had no answer for her, because honestly, what could I say?

That was not the end of the catty high school girl syndrome. Another girl who had seen me and Dean out on a date asked "What did you do to get him"? I guess she was implying that I was not good enough for him and I was probably having sex with him. That was the only conclusion my mind could come up with.

This barrage of negativity was taking its toll. One of the things I liked to do was escape this idle unproductive chatter was to go out into the field to a place where I felt small and the world was big. I would sing as loud as I could, dance, and skip till I was too tired to go on anymore, then just lay in the grass gazing at the clouds in the blue sky.

Another place of refuge was creating art. I liked to draw or paint to express and focus my thoughts. As a little girl, it was very difficult to sit and listen to the stories being read to me. Instead of reading a story, my mom would draw pictures of a princess, king, horse, ballerinas, and a myriad of other characters to entertain me.

She had wanted to be a commercial artist as a young woman, but became a secretary instead. Her skills supported the family business until it became prosperous enough for her to quit her job as a secretary. These changes all happened before my oldest brother Joe was born.

Her creativity was employed in designing flowers. She would create some of the most beautiful cut-flower arrangements I had ever seen. We would go to conferences where she would learn the latest designs for the flowers that were available on the market for making bouquets. One of those arrangements had a helium balloon attached with ribbon to a basket making a whimsical display of flowers look like it was about to go up in a hot air balloon.

She was able to use her skills to make posters with her drawings, letting people know what the specials were with each season change. Spring was the busiest time of the year for her. As exhilarating as each day was for her, she was exhausted from the constant activity. I would try to help, but was falling short on doing things quite right. She was so efficient and fast in how she approached the tasks that needed to be done, so my help would often be a hindrance to her routine of accomplishing the most pressing tasks.

I started to spend much more of my time drawing as I got older. Taking those childhood drawings my mother had made for me and trying to replicate them. My characters had big heads and little bodies. I could not figure out the proper proportions, so I created funny people. Making balloon letters for words was another fun thing as they were colored with bright magic markers. In ninth grade I started drawing still life displays such as driftwood, shells, and even a motorcycle helmet were some of the objects I sketched.

So I continued to create over the next three years. One oil painting was completed on a rather large canvas. The painting was created from a drawing I made over the summer. It was a rather odd creature with tentacles, meant to be menacing, but by the time I had finished it looked like a harmless dragon. Somehow, the fierce nature of my fictional beast was not translating well with a background of clouds that gave this creature a somewhat celestial appearance. That was not the original intent, but it was what it became.

The next painting was made from a designed drawing of an eye. There were flames above the eye, with cascading fields below the eye and waves on the bottom. My art teacher, Mr. Jonas, thought the drawing was quite curious and would be an interesting painting. He supplied me with another large canvas, which I prepared to paint with gesso. A quick sketch was made on the canvas and a palate of numerous colors were chosen to bring this black and white drawing to life. Other students were working masterfully on paintings that began as drawings as well.

There was a show scheduled for the middle of April and our paintings would need time to dry. While we were working on our various projects for the upcoming event our teacher Mr. Jonas would share a silly joke or make self-deprecating statements about his own idiosyncrasies. One day he had shared a joke, of which had totally gone over my head and I read nothing into it other than what was said.

My hiking advisor and teacher Mr. Ard had popped his head in the room and I shared the joke with him, "what goes in hard and red and comes out soft and pink", pause, "bubblegum". He laughed at the joke and left to get on with his next activity. After his departure, Mr. Jonas was fuming at his desk; he was upset with me for sharing the joke. He had to explain to me the deeper implications of the joke. After his explanation, I was extremely embarrassed of my naivety. I began to wonder what the other teacher thought who I had just told the joke to.

I had become rather introspective and began to worry too much about what other people thought. My friend, Karen, from the art class was a year younger than me and we did things outside of school together, be it a concert, dance, or movie. Her perspective on my current demeanor was that everything was happening all at one time. Finishing up artwork, classes, and tests were overwhelming me. I appreciated her taking the time to listen and talk through the situation and help me find peace.

Finding peace was one thing we did on Sunday mornings as a family. We went to Sunday school, but not church. If I wanted to stay for church my parents gave me permission to drive myself. One Sunday a discussion started on abortion. We had two teachers, a man and a woman, they just listened and did not offer their personal opinions. There was one very vocal participant, Shawn, who said that abortion was murder and there was no other way to explain it. I became the advocate for abortion and said women have a right to what goes on with their bodies.

He said, "They should have thought about that before they put another person's life at risk, and women would have to take responsibility for their actions." I said, "What about women who have been raped where they did not have a say in what was forced upon them?" He said that, God's grace would cover the women in those circumstances and he believed that abortion was still wrong.

Things were getting pretty heated and there were quite a few people just watching to see what the outcome would be. I was hoping the teachers would give us some inclination as to their personal thoughts on this controversial issue, but none was given. We continued back and forth on the issue until the end of class where Shawn shared the verse from Psalm 139, verses 13-14 KJV: "For thou hast possessed my reins: thou hast covered me in my mother's womb. I will praise thee; for I am fearfully and wonderfully made: marvelous are thy works; and that my soul knows right well".

That verse was a pretty compelling argument that God knew us in our mothers' wombs. But, is there a time early in a pregnancy where this is null and void because the tissue has no form or substance? There were still a lot of questions that had no conclusive answers in my mind. I was disappointed that the teachers did not interject their particular views to help us formulate an answer. What once was wrong, was now being touted as right. How were we to know the truth on an issue if there were no absolutes?

That Sunday left me in a quandary of thoughts. Was it right or was it wrong? I had two friends who already had abortions and part of me thought: why not? It was legal. What would their lives look like if they had the child? What ramification would all this have on them physically and mentally?

These topics had not been explored to the best of my knowledge. Was the fetus a baby or not? This all left me disquieted as to why would something be legalized if it was so wrong? Life goes on and each day has its own set of difficulties and I would have to put these thoughts to the back of my mind, for life was happening.

Monday morning started with my Algebra 2 class. Mr. Allen, the teacher, was going around the room pointing out those individuals who needed to take the class again because he felt they did not have a good grasp of the concepts he had taught. He had gone around the room and came to me and said, "you are one of those individuals who should take the class again". I said, "I will not be here, I am graduating".

Mr. Allen began to lecture about life and assuming responsibilities. He asked, "Are you ready to experience the real world?". I was not failing his class and my goal was to pass. His speech was a bit embarrassing as I was singled out to be given a pep talk on life. Maybe what he said had some merit and should have been taken a little more seriously.

The week had flown by quickly and Saturday was here. I had tried to prepare the best I could for the SAT's. It was early in the morning and the test was being proctored at another nearby school. The school district had just built a new high school. It consisted of three large circular buildings. They had a nickname for the buildings, the "three ring circus". I wasn't sure what door to go in so I just followed the other students whom I assumed were there for the test as well.

The man in charge of our room for testing took the attendance by calling out the name of each individual. My name was called and I responded: "here." We were supplied with a test and a number two lead pencil. We were given instructions and told that each portion of the test had a particular time limit and that we should pace ourselves accordingly to each subject.

Before each part of the test, he would have us go to the correct page and tell us to begin. When the time for that section was over he would instruct us to put our pencils down. There was reading, writing, language, and I found myself trying to make calculated guesses because I was not sure what the answers actually were. The pressure was mounting as the test progressed. Math was the final portion of the test and it started out pretty well.

I seemed to have a good grasp of the problems presented on the test. There was an increasing nature to the difficulty of the equations, but my organic chemistry class had prepared me well for this type of processing. I thought this would be the most trying part of the test and it proved not to be. When the time for the test was over, the proctor instructed us to bring our tests and pencils to his desk in the front of the room. He informed us that the results would arrive in the mail in about six weeks.

The next six weeks seemed so far away! I needed a good score, because there was no Plan B, so the pressure was mounting. Maybe I should have been more studious over the past eleven years. I had a reputation for not doing well. After taking a test in class the other students would ask what my grade was to make sure they did better than me. Could I possibly hope for the desired results that were needed?

33

"Everything you can imagine is real."

- Pablo Picasso

CHAPTER 4
APRIL - PLANNING

The news was reporting that Howard Hughes had died on Monday, April 5th. He was an eccentric individual who had been in the media for years. He had tried his hand at many creative projects and made a lot of money. He was known to be one of the wealthiest men in the world. Today's news brought to the forefront the realization that money can't bring health and happiness.

Howard Hughes enjoyed a multifaceted and exciting life. He had many business ventures in New York City and my high school art club was taking a field trip there to see the Guggenheim and the Metropolitan Museum of Art. I had not been to New York City in seven years and was a bit apprehensive.

When I was nine years old I went on a bus trip with my mother and her friend Alice. It was Christmas time and the crowds were so thick that I was taken along with the mob from my mother and was unable to find her. I approached a police officer and told him that I had been separated from my mother. He took me and walked up and down the line of busses and we eventually found my mom on the bus. This experience left an inward fear of the big city. Today was an opportunity to dispel my previous anxiety.

We all filed onto a coach bus for this trip, no yellow school bus today. When we arrived at The Metropolitan Museum of Art we were greeted by massive displays of art from all time periods. We got to see the masters up close, such as Leonardo da Vinci, Rembrandt, Caravaggio, and Michelangelo. Their work was astounding in the complexities and details that were painted with such precision. Even though the paintings were hundreds of years old, the colors were still vibrant. They had a hall filled with artists from the Impressionist era with the likes of Van Gogh, Degas, Renoir, Monet, and Mary Cassatt to name a few. There were sculptures and the modern art section showed the work of Andy Warhol.

Lunchtime came and we headed to the museum's cafeteria. There were so many choices of food that I had never seen or tried before. They had coffee yogurt which was a new food choice for me. My reasoning for choosing this was that I loved coffee ice cream. I was soon to find out that yogurt is not like ice cream. It was unsweetened and creamy, but was also very sour. I also had a sandwich made with multi-grain bread, I never had this type of bread before.

After lunch we were off to our next stop in the Big Apple, the Guggenheim Museum of Modern Art. The building captured my attention more than the artwork showcased within. The circular ascending ramps were like nothing I had ever seen before. Frank Lloyd Wright created this extraordinary building on the Upper East Side of Manhattan.

It took him sixteen years to complete this structure, finishing up the year I was born, 1959. The spacious interior offered a unique view as you looked up to the top of the building. Once I walked up to the ramp the view down was even more ominous. The artwork paled compared to this building which I considered the true testament to Frank Lloyd Wright's ingenious design.

We had a busy day and were loading onto the bus to go home. I had many thoughts of the works of art I had personally never seen before like Jackson Pollock, Francisco Goya, Paul Gauguin, Pablo Picasso, Wassily Kandinsky and so many other artists that it put my mind in overload and I could not process the wide array of art styles and composition.

In one of my childhood books it read: "The world is so full of a number of things, I think we should all be as happy as Kings". After a day like today, it helped broaden my mind as to the possibilities of what the world has to offer to each one of us. So much beauty and so much to entertain and enjoy. I would have to get my feet on the ground, take life a moment at a time and not dream about what could be, or could I?

Our works of art were taken to the local college for a display in their art gallery for the local art show. The clay pots and sculptures were displayed on high tables, the drawings had been matted before they were hung on hooks by thin metal wire that had been attached to the back of the mats. The paintings were placed on pegs that were already on the walls from previous shows. The artwork that would win awards in this show would move on to a state competition and if you won in the state event you moved onto a show that featured artwork by students from all over the United States.

We all had high hopes, but the final decision was with a group of judges from the college who were seasoned in choosing the best pieces to represent the talent from our area of the state. Mr. Jonas had gotten my hopes up and he was very excited about my paintings, they were very different and a bit eccentric.

The day of the show came and we were all wondering what the outcome would be. Some beautiful drawings, a few pieces of uniquely glazed pottery, and some photography took the prize to advance to the state level. Mr. Jonas was so disappointed that my paintings did not make the cut that he asked the judges why. They pointed out a few things they did not like about the paintings and it helped him understand their decision. He felt compelled to tell me why the paintings fell short of their standards. At that point I realized he was actually more disappointed than I was.

Should I cross off the goal of becoming a great artist? I may have been knocked down, but I would continue to draw and paint because it was a place of great joy for me. My boyfriend Dean would encourage me to pursue art as a hobby and maybe not as a career. That was some helpful advice to keep me focused on the important things and not be discouraged.

That weekend I got together with Dean. My parents were gone for the day and as evening settled in the house it became chilly inside. We had lived in the house for over eleven years and it had two fireplaces that we never used. Dean's house had a fireplace that they used frequently throughout the winter. He had a working knowledge of how to use a fireplace and he took this opportunity to break ours in.

We had some wood out back that we brought in and placed in the fireplace. He had some kindling which he used to start the larger logs on fire. He opened the damper to let the smoke out, but instead the smoke came furling back into the house. We started to open doors and windows for the smoke to make its way outside. Our efforts to dissipate the smoke seemed feeble. It was becoming so thick in the house that we could not see.

He came to the realization that our chimney was blocked and the smoke could not get out. He worked to extinguish the fire and get the smoke to move out the windows and doors we had opened. The smoke was harsh and made our eyes water as we continued to wave the smoke to areas for it to exit. After a time the smoke began to dispel, but the smell was still pretty strong throughout the house.

The air freshener that was used had met its match. As things cooled down we noticed a wall in another room on the other side of the fireplace had cracked. So not only did the house smell bad, there was now a cracked wall to explain.

After all the fire excitement our activities took a turn as the fire of lust took hold. We went down a road I had never gone before, but my curiosity and deep feelings of love lured me into uncharted waters. You explain these times away with the thinking, "I'm going to marry him anyway". I was deeply disappointed with myself. The guilt and shame seemed to consume my thoughts. I was feeling so uncomfortable with myself and unsure if there was any redemption from my sin.

Being a quiet and shy person it was difficult for me to express my thoughts. The Bible calls it fornication. I started to take a closer look at what this book had to say about this matter and found in Deuteronomy 22:28-29: "If a man meets a virgin who is not betrothed and seizes her and lies with her, and they are found, then the man who lay with her shall give to the father of the young woman fifty shekels of silver, and she shall be his wife, because he has violated her. He may not divorce her all his days."

The Bible also says if we confess our sins God is faithful and just to forgive us. I sought His forgiveness. My mother had said previously, "good girls don't do that". As much as I wanted to talk to her, I was too ashamed to tell her what had happened. I can only speculate that it would have been a difficult conversation. Life and events were happening and I just tried to move on.

Tickets were going on sale for the prom. I asked Dean if he wanted to go and he said, "yes". I purchased two tickets and all I needed was a dress. My friend Kate had a great sense of style and I asked if she would come with me to find the right dress. We left on Saturday morning to go to a large mall about two hours away from home. I did not like shopping and was looking forward to having her help.

We got to the mall; she had a few things she was looking for herself so we went to some stores to see the items she was hoping to find. Four hours and six stores later we arrived at the store where she thought we would find just the right dress. We got a couple of dresses off of the displays which I took back to the dressing rooms. I came out with a lavender and light blue dress with a pink floral swirl pattern. It was smocked at the top with an a-line skirt. The back and front came down into a rounded V shape. It had long, puffy sleeves and was like a beautiful gypsy dress. This would be the dress we both agreed was the most flattering.

That encounter of shopping for hours was not a pleasant experience for me. Most women love to shop, but I do not have the patience to endure the time spent going from store to store and this trip only increased my dislike of shopping. I now go in, get what is needed and leave.

The weekend after our shopping trip, there was a party at a cabin in the woods. The cabin was pretty big with a common area where everyone seemed to gather. There was an enclosed porch where a few of us met to talk about school and upcoming events. I didn't know many people there, but it seemed like an older group of people who had graduated a few years ago.

As we were talking, a scream and some crying came from inside. Kate, the friend who had helped me pick out the dress, was in distress. There were a few people trying to comfort her in the main area. She was wrought with anguish and had asked for someone to take her home. Someone said they would drive her there and they got in the car quickly and left.

We were unsure what happened and we chose to leave too. I later found out that she had been raped by a young man that evening. She was still visibly shaken the following week. The once bubbly and funny person was gone, like something had broken in her. I honestly didn't know how to help or what to say.

Dean and myself had a friend Lance who was a quadriplegic and was badly broken in a car accident when he was seventeen. Initially they thought he would not survive, as he sustained some serious head injuries. He was dependent on everyone to care for all his needs. Dean and I would go on dates with him to visit friends and attend gatherings as a threesome in his handicapped van. You had to listen closely to what he said, but he could articulate his thoughts very well.

Looking at Lance in the wheelchair and the joy he had for life, was so humbling. He had learned to use a ham radio and could talk to people all over. His life was such an inspiration as he rose from a dismal situation to embrace the possibilities with the support of his family, in particular his mother. He had a set of exercises he would do daily to keep what little movement he had intact. When he would laugh, his eyes twinkled and the sound of his laughter would come on the inhale.

I could be working with people like Lance if I became an Occupational Therapist and helping people recover from adverse situations. Not all people would be as optimistic as our friend and every individual situation is so different. Life can throw some curveballs and we all need to learn how to maneuver through the obstacles.

He helped me realize that each one of us has the potential to operate in a deep-seated joy. His mom worked hard, not only in his care, but also on their family farm. She would make the large meals for the farm hands and can the produce that was grown in the garden. Sometimes you learn a lot while watching other people's lives to see what you can emulate. His mom was a superwoman in my eyes.

"Happiness makes up in height for
what it lacks in length."
- Robert Frost

CHAPTER 5
MAY - READY, SET, GO

Pennsylvania had a businessman, and our first Jewish governor whose name was Milton Shapp. He was a champion for the disadvantaged. He served the state by bringing it back from almost becoming bankrupt. Our governor also became popular across the United States when he was the successful moderator in a truckers strike that was shutting down businesses across the country.

Governor Milton Shapp had decided in 1975 to run for President of the United States. He was popular with Pennsylvania residents, but that popularity did not translate into a nationwide appeal as he did not get the same media coverage as the other candidates. He had campaigned for eighty nine days before he dropped out of the race in May. He continued to finish his term as the governor of our state.

Only one president was from the state of Pennsylvania and that was James Buchanan. He was a lawyer and a politician that served as the fifteenth president between 1857 and 1861. This was right before the civil war started. He came from a large family with four brothers and six sisters.

My neighbor had six children and I used to play with them. There was never a dull moment. My grandmother was the oldest of ten children and had learned to be a responsible young woman. She had three children and eleven grandchildren. It was my birthday and she gave me a card with money in it.

A blueberry pie was in the oven baking, my favorite. My mother would make this instead of a birthday cake as far back as I can remember. I was turning seventeen and getting ready to graduate. I did not know how many blueberry pies she would be baking for me after this year.

One movie I had gone to the theatre to see with my mother

when I was a little girl was now on television; the 1965 hit, *The Sound of Music*. The drama in this movie was set during the time of World War II. The music and humor makes this a classic for all time. The song, "I Am Sixteen Going on Seventeen", was more than a song for me, but a reality. This young woman was so perplexed about her future just like me.

Another birthday gift came from Dean, a necklace. It was a black onyx pendant with a diamond in the center with a fine white gold chain. He let me know he really had no interest in going to the prom. He had bought two tickets to go see "Chick" Corea, an American jazz pianist and composer. The dress that I spent hours of my time shopping for would not be worn.

The tickets had been returned the week before the prom. We would be heading to the concert, a two hour drive to get to the venue. We had really good seats that were close to the stage. The musicians came onto the stage with Chick. His wife joined him on stage as well. He played a song that he had written for her to sing and her beautiful voice resonated through the atmosphere.

This was not a regular concert with glitzy lights or smoke, but the ambience of the evening was established by the tempo of the music. Some songs were upbeat with a short staccato beat and other songs were slow and melodious. What an incredible night to experience and remember.

There were so many things happening and the SAT test scores had arrived. They were well above what the school had required to be accepted. No more wondering, I would be headed off to college and it was all exciting at this time. When we were back at school on Monday everybody was sharing their test scores. I was asked what my score was and they could not believe I had done so well.

Focusing on finishing this last high school year well was now an attainable goal. The artwork that went to the college came back to our school. They had a local art show of the works that had been displayed. There were a few posters that had just been completed and were shown for the first time.

They also brought artwork over from the grade schools and middle school. There were drawings from the youth of George Washington, Uncle Sam, Abraham Lincoln, and many other iconic images commemorating our nation's 200th birthday. There were collages and American flags from different time periods in our nation's history. Each hallway in the school displayed different grade levels of work and classroom projects celebrating this unique period in time.

The display of artwork brought an award for one of my paintings, first prize. Someone said the painting reminded them of a Salvatore Dali painting. I took that as a compliment, but it was nothing like the genius style of Dali, that was known as surrealism. He was a bit eccentric and his work was very thought-provoking. One of my favorites was the one that looked like melting watches.

A picture of my painting would be printed in a publication that came out at the end of the school year. This book was compiled from hundreds of works by students from all grade levels. These projects were submitted by the teachers and a panel of judges determined what would be included in this publication. There was photography, drawings, stories, and poetry.

There was a poem I wrote in one of my English classes that was going to be published as well. When I read over the poem, which I had forgotten I wrote, the content surprised me:

THE WHOLE FEELING

YOU CAN SMELL ME: The aroma of spices and
     Seasoning caresses the atmosphere.
YOU CAN HEAR ME: Laughter colliding with the
     singing in the kitchen.
YOU CAN FEEL ME: Warm and soft and
     Seemingly unreal.
YOU CAN TASTE ME: Juices being savored.
YOU CAN SEE ME: Smiles aglow, trees and
     Tinsel, lights on the blink.
AND YOU CAN THINK OF ME: Born to save men from sin.

I had accepted Jesus when I was eleven and was baptized on Palm Sunday of that year. I was not living up to the standards in the Bible, it's called compromise. I liked to talk about Jesus. I allowed the thoughts of others to influence the things I said and did. It says in the Bible about being tossed to and fro by every wind and wave of doctrine.

One of the ways I was falling short was not helping my mom around the house the way I should have and thought mowing the yard was my only responsibility. I would put on my wrangler overalls, fill up the gas tank and take off for an hour long trip of mind-numbing activity. Sometimes I'd go over things that should not have been mowed and bent the lawn mower blades. There was a need to take responsibility in doing a job well.

The next weekend would be a trip with the hiking club from school. We would be going along the river banks of a fifteen mile trail that looped around in a circle. We would be backpacking and sleeping outside. I had a good pair of hiking boots that were comfortable. This would be my first overnight hike and we would be cooking over an open campfire. Our two advisers, Mr. Ard and Ms. Deck would be taking seven other students and myself. I was the only female student along with our advisor Ms. Deck.

We left early Saturday morning around four to get to the trail by nine o'clock. We headed into an area that had much higher mountains and more dense forest than I had ever seen. When we got to the beginning of the trail there were markers at eye level so we could easily navigate along the path. It was late spring, everything was so lush and green. There were some white flowers that looked like stars amongst the ground cover.

We started by going up a steep incline and the group stayed together for a time until there were a few of us who started to lag behind. It was a clear crisp day with a steely blue sky and the puffy animated clouds that changed into a variety of shapes. The higher up we went, the more colorful the riverbed became. It was some thirty feet between us and the river's bottom. We were walking along a steep cliff. The slate below was brilliant reds and greens. The water was so crystal clear as it washed over the rocks.

We continued on the trail for several hours and came to a very high pinnacle. As we looked up we saw a very large bird drifting on the wind. He began to fly closer to our location and we were able to see him up close. Our advisor identified this large raptor as a Golden Eagle. It was so majestic as it floated on the streams of air and we admired its beauty. We enjoyed the presence of this large bird for some time before it flew away.

The trail started to descend and we could still look over the side of the trail and see the colorful riverbed. We took a rest break and figured we had another four hours until we reached the area where we would be camping. Now was the time to persevere despite the long way to go as our initial enthusiasm had waned. Before we knew it, we arrived and met the other members of our group to set up camp for the night.

We set up our tents on level areas and rolled our sleeping bags out inside. My sleeping bag was new and the label assured warmth even if it got as cold as 32 degrees Fahrenheit. Someone had already started a fire and we all had dehydrated meals that we added water to and then heated them over the fire in our little cook pots. We had canteens for water and Mr. Ard made some instant coffee. Ms. Deck also had a curious goat cheese that was brown and tasted pretty sweet, almost like candy.

As we sat around the fire we shared our experiences. Some who moved ahead of our group had missed the Golden Eagle. We talked about the colorful riverbed and the difficult areas where it was hard to maneuver over some of the large boulders. There was some joking, storytelling, and we were soon off to our tents. I had my own, but the boys had two in each tent.

My sleeping bag was warm and I fell right asleep. In the morning someone had started a small fire to heat water for oatmeal, tea, or coffee. After breakfast the fire was put out and we rolled up our sleeping bags, took down our tents and packed everything up into our backpacks to head back to the van.

We were going on one short hike to a nearby trail before heading home. When we arrived at the entrance to this trail, the trees in this wooded area were huge. They said that the trees had never been touched and they were known as a virgin forest. We spent a short time exploring this area that was truly magical.

We hopped in the van after our short hike and pulled out for the long ride home. Our advisors shared some of their life experience, with us and it was really interesting. I fell asleep somewhere along the way. It was a Sunday and we would be going back to school the next day. This was a nice break and a good time to reflect on what's important in life.

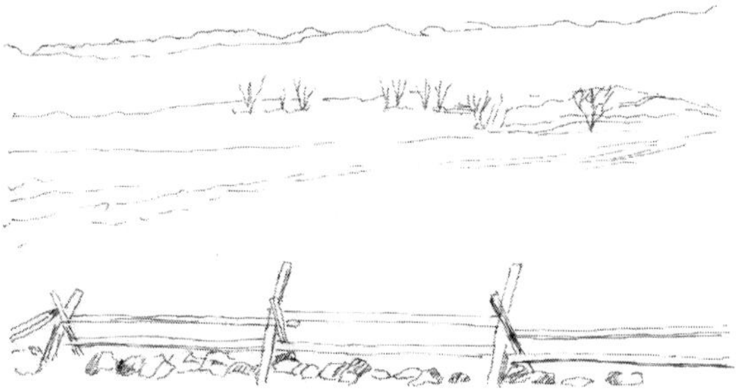

"Folks are usually about as happy as they make their minds up to be."

- Abraham Lincoln

CHAPTER 6
JUNE - GRADUATION

This was the final week of high school. Everyone was busy cleaning out desks, lockers, and picking up gowns and mortarboards that were ordered over three months ago. The yearbooks were handed out and everyone was writing messages to each other in them. All my grade school comrades would be graduating next year. It's hard to believe I spent twelve years with them since kindergarten.

The teachers were calculating final grades and expressing their heartfelt wishes for success in the future. It all seemed a bit unreal. There were many who had taken advanced placement classes. They had worked very hard and were diligent in taking purposeful steps to advance into their desired professions.

Some went to the vocational technical school to learn a skill, while others already had jobs. There were those working while learning a trade through their experience on the job. A few students had started using various drugs and would struggle with life. We all felt the pressure and dealt with it the best we could.

One of the classes I had at the end of this year was showing a series of films by Francis Schaeffer, *"How Should We Then Live?"* This series of films gave an overview of the history of the world. By the end of the series, many riveting questions were being addressed about the disintegration of the moral fabric of our country and the world. The only plumb line for any culture was from the Bible. There was much to consider as to how we could possibly live apart from the principles of God.

There was a news story about a young woman who had taken valium and alcohol at a friend's birthday party. She hadn't eaten anything for a while and became faint, her friends checked on her a little later and found she wasn't breathing. An ambulance was called and mouth-to-mouth resuscitation was performed and she became conscious, however, later she went into a coma and was put on a ventilator.

Her parents had been seeking to have her taken off the ventilator and they filed a suit, which was eventually granted this month. Once off the ventilator, she was able to breathe on her own and a feeding tube was placed. Her parents said they wanted her in as natural a state as possible so she could die in God's time.

This case had caused a controversy throughout churches and culture. The debate was on and there were no clear answers. Drugs were a bane in our culture and lives were being destroyed by them. Some of it may have been peer pressure; I know I succumbed to this and had tried marijuana and alcohol. Another group of youth were using drugs to dull emotional and physical pain in their lives. These were some of the unfortunate realities in some of the students' lives.

Our graduating class was getting ready for the baccalaureate service. The local pastors joined together for Bible readings, messages, and singing. This service was held in the school's auditorium. We had a rehearsal of how we would file in for seating before the actual service. The night of the service we wore our gowns and mortarboards. We entered as we had rehearsed.

When I got home that evening, my mother explained how she was so disappointed with my poor posture. To be honest, I had never thought about my posture before this. I began to formulate a plan to remedy my posture problem. For graduation it was good to know that I had to stand taller. I don't know where the idea came from, but would ballet classes help my posture?

The night of graduation was here, grandparents, parents, and friends were sitting in the bleachers to watch the class receive diplomas. The football field was the stage where we would sit. I wore a light dress and comfortable shoes so I would not get so hot. I felt bad for the boys in their shirt, ties, and pants they wore under their gowns. Even though it was early in the evening, it was still pretty hot.

We were given a white carnation to put on the lapels of our robes. Mortarboards were in place on our heads with the tassels to the right. We filed out by two abreast and there was a palatable tension in the air as the band played. The valedictorian was named for the class and gave an encouraging word to us all.

A special guest speaker spoke and honestly I can't remember a thing that was said. The names of the graduates were being called out in alphabetical order. Special honors were being bestowed upon those who studied and worked hard over the years. As we received our diplomas we moved our tassels to the left on our mortarboards.

The superintendent got up to give the closing remarks and announced the class of 1976. There was a roar that sang out over the crowd of people as hats went flying. Everyone started to look for family members. Photos were being snapped with Kodak Instamatic and Polaroid instant film cameras. People were hugging and crying. I found my grandparents as they were waiting at the base of the bleachers to congratulate me.

The following Monday, I called the nursing home to get a schedule for volunteering. They said if I wanted to come every day between ten in the morning till lunchtime that it would be a great help for them. I was hoping this would give me some experience in how to care and help others. I would be assisting older people with simple tasks. I told them I would be in the following week to start.

There was another activity I wanted to look into before I went to college, my posture. I looked in the yellow pages for someone who taught ballet. I have never seen a ballerina with bad posture. I called one of the numbers and I explained my purpose for wanting to learn ballet. She said, "Since you are an older student with no experience, a private lesson would probably be the best option". So we set up a weekly class at her home studio to learn some basic ballet moves. She told me to get a dance leotard which was an all-in-one shirt with holes for my legs, arms, and head.

I went to the first class at her home, where she taught me how important the positions of the arms, feet, and body were. She used a wall mirror so I could see what I was doing. Ballet is based on fundamental movements. The first move she taught me was the plié. I had to keep both feet flat on the floor at all times and bend my knees.

Relevé was the next move she showed me how to do. My feet were together and my knees were kept straight while I would lift my heels. Arabesque is a position where I would stand on one leg and stretch out the other leg straight behind my body. The standing leg could be bent or straight, but my back leg had to be straight.

The class consisted of me doing these movements repetitively for some time. I was gaining an appreciation for the strength and flow that the ballerinas had. I was just learning the simple basic moves, but my teacher believed that if I practiced them on a regular basis my posture would improve. There is a discipline and accuracy that must be established through the movements for them to have any benefit.

My friend Karen called and was wondering if I wanted to go to a dance with her. No ballet tonight. I told her I would pick her up after supper. We were headed to an outside pavilion where a local band was playing. It took us about twenty minutes to get there and as we pulled into the area there were no parking places. The event was really full and we had to park up on the next street.

As we walked down the sidewalk, we talked about the plans we had for the next few weeks. I told her my parents were taking in an exchange student for a few weeks and I would have to sleep on the sofa. Karen said, "Where is she from?" I said, "She's from Italy, we had a girl from Mexico last year. My parents had someone come and serenade her." She said, "That sounds like you had a good time with her."

It was a balmy Friday night and the music was loud as the sound seemed to hang in the air. It's good the dance was outside, because it would be hard to contain the crowd of people that showed up.

We didn't know anyone there so we spent some time watching the people and listening to the music.

We decided to dance and some of the locals started to talk to us. We had to talk really loud to hear each other over the music. We found out that two of them had graduated recently from high school. They asked if we would be coming next week and we told them we would. The group played their last song and we headed back to the car. Karen asked, "Are we really going to go back next week?" I asked, "Did you have fun?" Karen answered, "Yes". So it was established that we would go back next week.

We were almost home when we came upon a curious sight. There were two people standing by the side of the road and two in our lane holding a chain. My heart began to pound as I asked Karen to, "Close your window and lock your door". My hands were shaking as we approached them. Honestly I did not know if they needed help or were there to harm someone. We were too scared to ask.

As we got closer they moved off the road and we passed by with nothing happening. We began to relax and take a deep breath as we thought we averted a major catastrophe. That whole scenario is a mystery as to why they were there. We were glad it was not what it appeared to be.

Our exchange student would be arriving and the final preparations were being made to make her comfortable. The young lady from Mexico had been so vibrant and fun to be with and talk to. This student was from Italy and the experience would be totally different.

Sophia was dropped off by a member of the group that was sponsoring her visit to the United States. She had sleek dark hair and was very elegant. The dark green dress she wore accentuated her hazel eyes. Her olive complexion highlighted her fine facial features, giving the impression that she was somewhat aloof.

My bed for the next few weeks would be the sofa. The only thing that bothered me about that was the lack of privacy. She would be traveling with the sponsors to see various sights in the United States. Her first visit would be to Washington D.C., our capital, and later she would be traveling to New York City.

She had a full schedule and my parents would be taking her on a few day trips to see the local attractions. One day my brother Joe gave her a ride on his new motorcycle. She did not straddle the seat with her legs, but perched both legs to the right side of the bike. We had not seen anything like this in person before. He told her to hold on tight and they were off for a ride.

While staying with us she had made plans to stay with another family, so she was not going to be with us for as long as we had originally thought. I had heard she was part of the Communist Party, I wasn't even sure what that meant. No one from my family had said this, but it was something I picked up in her conversation.

There were three communist countries that I could think of: the USSR (Union of Soviet Socialist Republic), China, and Cuba had become a communist country the year I was born. None of these countries seemed to be proponents of freedom. The news would talk about the cold war between the United States and the Soviet Union. In 1972 President Nixon went to China so our countries would have better relations with one another.

"I predict future happiness for Americans, if they can prevent the government from wasting the labors of the people under the pretense of taking care of them."

-Thomas Jefferson

CHAPTER 7
JULY - 200th YEAR CELEBRATION

When we look back on our history, we think of George Washington and Thomas Jefferson who wrote the Declaration of Independence, which was accepted by the Continental Congress and voted on July 2nd, (my mom's birthday) but would be celebrated July 4th, 1776. The thirteen American colonies made it clear through this document that they would no longer be part of England. The battles of Lexington and Concord were the first battles in the war for independence. Many years passed since the American Revolutionary War had begun and ended in 1783.

These events were cause for celebration 200 years later with parades taking place in many communities, picnics, and of course, fireworks at many locations throughout the country. There was a Wagon Train that started in the state of Washington on June 8, 1975, and came clear across the country to finish the trip at Valley Forge, Pennsylvania on July 4, 1976. The President, Gerald Ford, would be throwing the first pitch for the All Star Major League Baseball game and there were so many activities to choose from to celebrate this monumental occasion.

My parents were celebrating their twenty-fifth wedding anniversary, so they were married when our country was 175 years old. They had a picnic at our house, which was catered, and they had all their employees, friends, and family in attendance. It was a sunny beautiful day and my mom had games for the children and volleyball for the adults.

They set up the garage with an air conditioner to keep the food fresh. Everything was ready for people to easily get what they wanted to eat, like a cafeteria. She had purchased prizes for the winners of the games and a rousing game of bingo was played, which added to the suspense for everyone. The volleyball game was pretty competitive as people were jumping and diving to keep the ball going from side to side. My mom was an organizational pro and had planned a great time of celebration for everyone!

The next day was Monday and I would be going to the nursing home to help with the activities. We would make a simple craft for their rooms or to give to friends or family. Sometimes, I would stick around and help get lunch for the residents. Some would like to talk about times past; it was an interesting local history lesson. Some liked to sing and it gave them all so much joy!

I was never in a situation like this, helping other people, before. Not having any younger siblings or learning how to care for others. I felt like I gained more from meeting and knowing these people than what I did to help them. It was a surprise and relief that I actually enjoyed helping people.

Last summer I had worked at an ice cream stand making sundaes, milkshakes, cones, and root beer floats as my job. Even though I was not getting paid for volunteering, it was a more rewarding experience than serving ice cream. Although I really enjoy ice cream, the new experiences in volunteering was proving to be more gratifying!

The 1976 Summer Olympics would be off and running in Montreal, Quebec, Canada. I really enjoyed following the events and could not fathom the time and energy that was expended for each athlete to reach this point in their lives. There were ninety-two countries participating and Queen Elizabeth II was there to open the games. There were many events in twenty-one sports. Some of my favorites were swimming, diving, fencing (which I had tried when I was in eighth grade), gymnastics, track, and field competitions.

One person who really got our attention was Bruce Jenner. He won the Olympic gold medal with a new world record of 8,618 points. My mom and I found ourselves rooting for Jenner as each of his events took place. It was the ease and grace which he seemed to conquer each challenge with unflappable stamina and strength.

He had to accomplish a lot in the decathlon featuring ten events including the pole vault, high jump, long jump, javelin, shot put, discus, 110 meter hurdles, 100 meter dash, 400 meter run and a 1500 meter run. At the end of all these challenges Jenner came out as the winner and my mom thought he was the best-looking champion.

Another record breaking athlete was the Romanian gymnast Nadia Comaneci. She was the first woman to score a perfect 10 as an Olympic gymnast in the 1976 games and she was just fourteen years old. Her amazing routines were breathtaking. It was hard to believe that someone could be so precise in the execution of the floor exercise, the balance beam, uneven bars, and vault. She won the Olympic gold medal for the individual all-around in gymnastics.

The United States of America had won a total of ninety-four medals and thirty-four of those were gold medals. The men's swimming team did really well with John Nabor winning four gold medals in swimming the backstroke, freestyle, and medley. One country that was small, but well represented at the Olympics, was Japan. Maybe I took notice of this country in particular because we had visited some greenhouses in California a few years earlier that were owned by Japanese Americans.

A man who had helped my Father in business had taken us to these greenhouses to see the plants they were growing. They had grafted a colorful round cactus on a thick green base cactus to create what they called a Moon Cactus. They were skeptical when outsiders came to visit and were unsure whether they wanted us on their property. My Dad's friend talked to them and told them that we just wanted to see what they were growing. They left us in to visit their business and see their beautiful garden.

I was not familiar with what had happened to the Japanese Americans during World War II until then. After we left, my Dad's friend explained about the internment camps that the Japanese

Americans had to go to after the attack on Pearl Harbor. This was a forced relocation into concentration camps ordered by President Franklin D. Roosevelt.

The majority of these Japanese Americans were United States citizens. They had been born and raised in this country and were business owners, factory workers, and valuable members of our society. All of a sudden, they were uprooted from their lives and forced to live in camps far from home.

This was a new part of American history for me; our country had been a melting pot of all nationalities. Their personal freedoms had been violated in that time of incarceration. They had considered this their country and they were falsely accused of fraternizing with the enemy. Trust is not something that could be given after such a grave betrayal. They picked up the pieces and re-established their lives.

The preamble to the constitution states, "We the People of the United States, in Order to form a more perfect Union, establish Justice, insure domestic Tranquility, provide for the common defense, promote the general Welfare, and secure the Blessings of Liberty to ourselves and our Posterity, do ordain and establish this Constitution for the United States of America." Our founding fathers had tried to create a fair and equitable country to all that would want to come and call this country home. They say history is doomed to repeat itself if we do not learn from the past. Looking at the past, it's easier to see our failures then at the time.

Some disturbing news about my childhood friend Mark came that he had been killed in an accident. His death sent shockwaves through our small community. I remember when Mark and myself were five years old and would play in his sandbox building roads and garages. We also watched color television together, as they were the only ones that I knew that had one.

We would watch cartoons in color on the sofa in the living room. His mom would make us a snack of cookies and milk. We would laugh and giggle as we ate. Looking back, I would have considered him my best friend as a small child.

He had been adopted by his parents as a baby. There was a young lady from my class who was pregnant and was putting her baby up for adoption. Before abortion was legal many women would choose this alternative. Many families who could not have children were thankful to be able to adopt children to raise as part of their families.

Mark was gone now and his parents were having a funeral; they loved him very much as he was their only child. They would have done anything to have him back. Their pain and anguish were apparent. Many came from our neighborhood to show their respects. It was shocking that a young life had ended so soon.

I was listening to a new tape I had just gotten by James Taylor. The song that was playing, "Don't Be Sad 'Cause Your Sun Is Down", brought me to a full sob, as the song encouraged one to carry on despite hard times. We have our memories of him in our hearts for the rest of our lives.

"Learn to value yourself, which means:
fight for your happiness."

- Ayn Rand

CHAPTER 8
AUGUST - OFF TO COLLEGE

This was an election year and our current president, Gerald Ford, would be running against the Georgia Governor, Jimmy Carter, known also for being a peanut farmer. I was only seventeen and you needed to be eighteen to vote. Jimmy Carter emphasized his Christian beliefs as he campaigned across the country.

Change would be happening for many students as we would be going off to college for the first time. I was wrapping up my final ballet class and would miss the discipline that it afforded me. Hopefully my posture was better from having learned ballet positions and standing straight. My leotard and ballet slippers would be put away for now.

Going to the nursing home to say goodbye to my new friends would be difficult. I had learned so much from their wisdom. Some were very old and there was a possibility that I may never see them again. I was hoping to get in a visit during the breaks from college.

After the farewells I was headed for a trip to the shore. Dean was getting a cottage there and we would be going with other friends. I asked my parents if I could go and they said it was all right as long as we would be there with others. This would be a nice vacation before school started. The drive to get there was long, sunny, and hot

When we arrived the cottage was not right on the beach, but close enough to easily walk there. When we opened the door there were grasshoppers all over on the floor. They were alive and hopping everywhere. We got a dustpan, broom, and started to sweep them up to take these critters outside. There were so many of them everywhere, I had never seen anything like this before.

When we had taken care of our infestation, we made plans together for meals and activities we would do. The next morning, we had decided to go deep sea fishing. This would be a first time for me and the boat went very far out in the ocean, to the point where you could not see land. The water was pretty choppy and I was about to experience another first; getting seasick. Many others started having the same symptoms.

Despite the nausea many of us experienced we continued with the fishing expedition. The first fish I caught was a small bass. I looked at Dean and asked, "How old do you think it is?" He laughed and assured me I could throw it back into the ocean because it was too small. We had another hour out in the ocean before the boat headed back to the dock. That was one of the longest hours that I ever had to endure.

Somehow eating the fish after this adventure did not seem so appetizing. Gutting and cleaning the fish gave me a new appreciation for the market where you bought it cleaned and ready to eat. We dusted the filets with flour and fried them in a pan with oil. The fried fish that came out of the pan were pretty tasty.

The others in the group had to leave and go home. That left Dean and I there alone. We spent our last day on the beach, building a pyramid, and sphinx. Dean was out enjoying the waves in the ocean. There was a pod of dolphins swimming beyond the waves as they jumped in and out of the ocean.

We headed home the next day and my parents were pretty upset. They had found out that the others had come home and we were there alone for a short time. I apologized and was thankful that they cared, but what more could I do. It was a lapse in poor judgement on my part.

It was time to move on and get ready to leave home. I went shopping with my Mom to pick up all the things needed to outfit a dorm room. There was a comforter, sheets, pillow, lamp and a hot pot to make tea or those pouches with dehydrated soup that you make by adding hot water. We also purchased notebooks, pens, and pencils.

Everything seemed to be coming together and my mother's organizational skills and foresight would help alleviate a lot of headaches for me in the future. I was getting a little nervous about the realization of leaving home; not knowing anybody there had created a lot of apprehension. I just didn't know how to plan or prepare for what was ahead.

There were questions like, would I make new friends? Maybe nobody would like me? Would I be able to accomplish the assignments and keep up with the reading that would be required? It was like a fresh start and nobody knew me so there were no preconceived expectations. The day to leave was quickly arriving and I was getting everything in place or should I say my Mom was making sure everything was in order.

I would be doing my own laundry for the first time, so she showed me how to sort laundry, what setting to use to wash certain weights, clothing colors, and how much detergent to use. Without her lesson on laundry, I probably would have put everything in one load, with bubbles, and multi-colored clothing.

I would be leaving early the next day to get there in time for orientation. We decided it would be a good idea to load up the car the day before so we would not forget anything. I would be using my brother Joe's car to make the trip out west.

This was the last night with my parents and they were taking me out for supper to one of my favorite places. The restaurant had a special that night; lobster tail, a baked potato with sour cream, and coleslaw. The meal came with a basket of hot buns that would melt in your mouth. We finished the meal with a delicious strawberry cheesecake for dessert.

It was nice to spend this evening with my Mom and Dad. They were still a little skeptical as to whether I was going to apply myself to accomplish the task set before me. I was going to have to figure out how to do it on my own without their encouragement.

The big day was here and I heard a series of light taps on my window. I went over to investigate and I pulled the curtain back to look out the window. There was Dean throwing pebbles at the glass panes. I went out to say goodbye to him before he headed off to work. After breakfast, my parents came out to the car to see me off and wave goodbye as my journey was just about to begin.

I was on my way with a long drive and plenty to think about. I was a little apprehensive about who I would be sharing my room with. The time seemed to fly by quickly as I went through each tunnel on the turnpike. It would not be too long until I arrived at my destination and new home.

I was pulling into the parking lot and someone met me at the car with a card and directed me to where to park. We were then pointed in the direction of the cafeteria for a meeting with all the freshmen. Some of the students would be roommates with their friends through predetermined living arrangements. The majority of us would be meeting our roommates for the first time.

Sister Clover was there to greet us and brief us on rules and regulations; this school was going to be so strict and have so many more rules than I had at home. We were assigned to a dorm and given a room number. I headed over to the building and proceeded to look for the number on the door that would be my quarters.

I opened the door and was greeted by my roommate, Jan, and her mother. We shared what our majors were and I found out she would be in the nursing program. Her mother was a nurse and her father was a doctor. They had a helicopter that her dad could fly. She was so fascinating and sweet all at the same time. Jan seemed to smile nonstop and was very happy.

Her mom left after saying goodbye and giving Jan a hug. We got busy choosing beds and getting our sides of the room set up with everything we brought. She lived close enough that her parents would be picking her up every weekend. I would be staying on the weekends and going home only for special events and holidays. We were both kind of shy, but we quickly learned a lot about each other and our families, including each other's likes and dislikes.

After we had some time to settle in, we were directed into

the buildings where we learned more about the programs we were there to attend. A syllabus was given to us for the major we had chosen. It outlined our class schedules, what days, times, and the places where we needed to be. Somehow knowing the structure and time table gave me a sense of security.

The day was winding down and we were sent to the cafeteria for supper, as this was to be a meet-and-greet event. Everyone seemed so nice and I was able to meet others in my program and establish an acquaintance with some of my class members. One of them was a little person by the name of Sadie. She stood a bit over three feet tall and had a roommate by the name of Daisy, who was her friend. They had planned to be roommates before they arrived and were from a neighboring county next to where I lived and they had the same major, Occupational Therapy.

I met a few other people in different programs. This was a women's college and everyone who was admitted was female. The faculty was predominantly women. All my teachers were woman, except one, and he was Father Jones.

Father Jones was the professor of The Contemporary Moral Problems class. At first, I thought this class was going to be boring; my preconceived ideals led me to believe that this class was an indoctrination into the Catholic faith. The other classes that were on my schedule were English, Anatomy and Physiology, and Psychology.

There was a curious sight with these three beautiful girls with blonde hair who were friends. They were tall, skinny, and they all dressed in the same style of clothing. Whenever I saw them on campus, they were together. They did not intermingle with us very much and they were attending the same program together to become executive secretaries. This was so interesting initially, but then they just became part of the daily scenery. They even seemed to move in a synchronized fashion as they glided from place to place.

The next day we were given the opportunity to explore the

campus on our own. They had some beautiful trails around the campus and I decided to take up jogging around the area on these trails. I was new to jogging and was surprised at how far I could actually run. Having problems with asthma as a child, I did not lose my breath now while running.

One day as I was coming off one of the trails, a student stopped me to let me know a young lady had been raped on the trail. Why was a warning not given so it would be known by all? Walking in public places would replace my short-lived jogging routine.

After this disquieting revelation, there was another new exciting revelation; my roommate whistled in her sleep. I woke up in the middle of the night and she was whistling. I asked Jan the next morning, "Are you aware of the fact that you whistled in your sleep?" She said, "No, are you kidding me, I whistle in my sleep?" We had a good laugh and each time I heard it in the middle of the night I would smile and go back to sleep.

"Life is what happens to us while we are making other plans."

- Allen Saunders

CHAPTER 9
SEPTEMBER - NEW BEGINNINGS

In the news an unmanned spacecraft, The Viking, had landed on Mars September third. One of the purposes of this trip was to get color images of the surface of Mars. Now, we would find out if there were little green men on Mars. There was a show in the sixties called, *My Favorite Martian*, where a Martian landed on Earth. Songs like "Rocket Man", by Elton John, "Life on Mars?" and "Space Oddity" by David Bowie brought music into the fray of the celestial universe too.

School had taken on its own alternate universe. In just a few weeks, one begins to have a routine of going to class, eating, and studying. I would study everyday to retain the information taught so I could understand the material in the future. This put me in a totally different vein of thought and deed. In college, a whole new persona came forth.

I was put in a preliminary English class because I had not tested well in the entrance exam. Having to take this class was a reckoning to not learning what I should have learned in high school. Our English teacher, Sister Davis, was a nun and she was there to help us to gain better writing skills. She informed us we would have the entire semester to work on a research paper. We could choose any topic to research, but she would have to approve the subject.

Even though I had college prep courses in high school, there was never an assigned research paper to do in any of those classes. This would be my first research paper and my subject was somewhat broad. I wanted to know what "happiness" was. She said my topic would be fine and the research began.

I was surprised at the mountains of books that focused on this very topic. Sister Davis was surprised that I had never written a research paper before. She assured me she would be available to walk me through the process. It was good to know that help was available.

Friday night was here and a local college was sponsoring a dance. I was the designated driver for our group since I was the only one on campus with a car. There was a band playing and the musicians were pretty good. We started dancing together. A male student from that school asked me, "Would you like to dance?", I said, "No." One of his friends asked my friend Lyn if I was a lesbian. She said, "No, she has a boyfriend."

Saturday came and I had a good handle on my school work with all the reading and writing that needed to be accomplished for the following week. My schedule was not as full as some of the other students. The day was spent cleaning, organizing, and doing my laundry. It was so quiet in the dorm this weekend.

My friend Kate from high school stopped by on Sunday to see if I wanted to go on a picnic. The weather was beautiful and I was so surprised to see her. She attended a college that was about thirty minutes away. There were two of her new friends with her, so we packed up and headed out for the afternoon.

The roads Kate was traveling on were unfamiliar to me. The ride over gave me an opportunity to get to know her new friends, Anita and Mary. We soon came to a wooded area with a reservoir nestled between two hills. Kate got a blanket and picnic basket out of her car and we followed her to a clearing in the trees. We all took a corner of the blanket and flicked it up in the air and brought it down to the ground.

We made ourselves comfortable and looked around at the beautiful scenery. Initially we did small talk, how school was going, did we like our teachers, and was the cafeteria food good? Kate began to talk about the night at the cabin when she was raped.

She asked me, " Were you there that night?" I said, "I was, but I never knew what to say to you about it."

She said, "It was a really difficult matter for me and I'm still working through it, I just can't believe something like that happened to me." She went on, " I have heard of people getting pregnant after being raped, at least that didn't happen to me." Anita tried to encourage her by telling her how strong she has been in moving forward with her life. Mary said, "You have such a great sense of humor that you use to buffer the bumps in your life."

We spent some time just absorbing the sunshine and looking at the sunbeams as they filtered through the trees. The reflection of the trees in the water would ripple when a wind blew through this little valley. We soon packed up and she dropped me off. I was glad to have this time with Kate to reflect, and more importantly, be refreshed.

The weekend was over and we were back to our classes. There was an opportunity to do some volunteer work at a nearby state school. They were looking for someone to assist the students with making clay pots. This sounded like a good learning experience, so I signed up.

On the first day I went to volunteer, I followed the directions that brought me to the large concrete block buildings. They were ominous, dark, and dreary. I walked to the front door, which I opened, and walked in. I saw things I had never seen before and there was an overwhelming smell of disinfectant.

There were young people walking around with what looked like football helmets. I explained to the person at the front desk that I had come to volunteer in the art therapy department. She proceeded to lead me through a series of rooms where there were small children in steel cribs that looked more like cages. I started to wonder if I was in the right place. There was a little girl in the corner who jumped out and hissed at me.

We finally made it to the art therapy room. The students were already there working on rolling coils with clay. I was introduced to the director of the program and his young female assistant. I was to find out over time that the assistant was there to do community service for an infraction with the law.

They filled me in on how I could help the class members with what they were doing. Providing feedback through conversation was pivotal to this program. The children seemed to thrive and love the interaction. These children were in a vastly un-home like atmosphere, but they were so happy despite their surroundings.

I marveled at these children; just to give you an example, the one day it was a little girl's birthday. She had received a birthday card in the mail from her family and was so ecstatic. Her smile filled the room. She had Down's Syndrome and her family was encouraged by their family doctor to put her in a state home. I was so overwhelmed by the experience that day. After I left I just sat in my car and cried.

This whole episode would haunt me for the weeks to come. That girl had such a profound impact on me. Maybe things looked dismal at this particular school, but I believe the people who were employed there were giving them the best care they could. They did focus on quality interaction with the children through kindness and love.

After volunteering in the art therapy department for several weeks, I was seriously considering changing my major. One of the programs that the college had to offer was Art Therapy. I talked to the young man who was in charge of the program at the state school. He said that art therapy was a relatively new, field and anyone wanting to pursue a career in it would need to have a masters degree of which he had just received.

I was excited about the possibilities. I was not sure what my parents would think about a change in majors. It seemed like a perfect match though. I loved art and was learning to sincerely appreciate helping people; making coil and slab pots with the children and the sense of accomplishments we all had when their pots were completed.

I gave my parents a call on the weekend and to let them know what I would like to do. Explaining to them about the opportunities that could be achieved by changing majors. They were still in disbelief that I was really enjoying school. They said I would probably fare better staying in the current program for now and make the change in the following school year.

The second semester line-up of classes for the art therapy program seemed more to my core interest. Being impulsive the thought of having to make a decision now to start that program the next semester. My parents just wanted to see me get through one semester at a time.

My track record was not very good on completing projects. There was a fence at home that was only half way stained. The yard would get mowed, but never trimmed. The dishes would be waiting for me to dry and put them away. This was their experience with me.

I was improving in getting things done, like reading ten or more chapters a night. There wasn't much time for pleasurable reading. I was actually enjoying the information in my psychology book about Pavlov's experiments with dogs or Freud's views on people's dreams. All this information was new to me and very fascinating.

There was no time to be bored and time management came into play. One of the papers I wrote was about my experience at the state school. My teacher was so touched by the graphic pictures that I created with words, that she encouraged me to continue to write. She said I had a gift that should be used. No one had ever encouraged me like this before.

During the weekend there was a concert at a neighboring college. We could receive a discount if we brought our school IDs. I was going to be driving a group of classmates and wanted to leave early so we could sit in the very front row. The musician that evening was Tom Chapin, Harry Chapin's brother.

We got there and the other girls had forgotten their IDs. I was a bit annoyed with them because they knew I wanted to sit in the front row. Giving them the keys to my car they left to go back and get their cards.

I went up and got my front row seat, right in the center. I was sitting alone for some time and they did not return. The auditorium was filling up quickly and I realized they would have to sit in the back. The lights started to dim and Tom Chapin came out to play his first song; it was a fun song that he had us sing along with him for the chorus.

After the song was over, someone ran up and gave him a piece of paper. He read over it, looked up, and read what was on the paper. This is what he said, "Kay, your keys are stuck in the ignition and we can't get them out, please help us." I was frozen to the seat and did not move. Tom said, "Kay, are you here?"

There was silence throughout the auditorium. He commented that the individual must be embarrassed. I slowly got up and walked to the back of the auditorium, everyone started applauding. When I got back to my friends they apologized profusely. We went to the car and got my keys out of the ignition. We headed back into the hall and sat in the back row to enjoy the rest of the concert.

───────────────────────

This weekend was coming to an end, but the next weekend was an open house for our families. After a week of classes, my parents would be coming to visit the college for the first time. The college had planned events and a special supper for all those who came. The faculty would be there to answer any questions they may have about the college.

My parents arrived in time for the information session. I used this as an opportunity for my parents to become acquainted with the Art Therapy program that was offered at the school. They were impressed by the presentations that were made that day. They asked, "Is the food always this good?" I said, "Yes, it is delicious."

They came over to my dorm room and asked my roommate, "Does she always keep it this clean?" She said, "She is the neat one and I am the messy one." This was a surprise to them, because I was a slob at home and didn't clean up after myself. They had a long drive ahead of them and we said our goodbyes and they were gone. I went back to my room to finish up some projects and study for a test on Monday morning.

In preparing for a new week I had goals to work towards. My Anatomy and Physiology class was the greatest challenge, but a good one. I had been preparing for a lab test. The teacher would put arrows pointing to a certain section of a bone. In this test we were required to name the bone and the indentations and projections that were pointed out by these small arrows.

Monday had arrived and many found this test to be quite difficult and were concerned after it was over. Our professor said she would have our grades to us by the next class. There had been so much information to learn and not just the name of the bone, but identifying actual parts on the bone. I had spent weeks studying for this test.

Later that week, she gave us back the test with our grades. I had gotten a ninety-seven percent, almost a perfect score. I couldn't believe it! Everyone started talking to each other about what grade they had gotten. I had the highest grade in the class and I realized at that moment you can redirect your future. You can literally take control of your life through learning. This should have been an epiphany for me in the first grade.

"Courage is the most important of all the virtues because without courage, you can't practice any other virtue consistently."

- Maya Angelou

CHAPTER 10
OCTOBER - AWAKENING

One interesting development was that Barbara Walters, a journalist, was hired as the first woman to co-anchor the evening news with Harry Reasoner. She was starting at ABC television and hopefully her employment there would lead to other women journalists being gainfully employed by other television stations in more visible positions. Some changes that were happening were good and encouraging.

Women were working hard and accomplishing the goals they had set out to achieve. The Equal Rights Amendment (ERA) was being championed so that women and men would have the same rights under the law. One big part of all this was for women to be paid the same amount as a man for doing the same job. The National Organization for Women (NOW) was also an advocate for women as they saw the discrimination between men and women through all walks of life.

These changes were helping women use their talents and skills to make advancements in many vocations. In my opinion the current structure of thought about women holding more prestigious positions within companies was taking a turn for the good. Companies were examining the qualifications of an applicant and not the gender.

Some thought that the principles in the Bible excluded women from pursuing a more aggressive career path. I was going to a Catholic college and was unsure what their stance was on women in the workforce. One class I was required to take was Contemporary Moral Problems. Somehow I was hoping this class would offer answers as to why there were so many injustices in the world.

They invited various groups from within the Catholic faith to come and share their information about the organizations they were affiliated with in working for social justice or spiritual enrichment. One group that came to share was a ministry that helped to feed the starving and dying people around the world. They made us aware of the magnitude of overwhelming needs throughout the entire world. Their encouragement to us was that if we all worked together, we could have a greater impact on helping the needy.

This topic was really overwhelming, but there are so many starving and dying people in the communities of third world countries. The problem seemed so far away as we lived in the land of good and plenty. Some governments created the difficulties for the people through impossible rules and regulations. The leadership of some countries dictated how they should live or even whether an organization could help them.

The next week two nuns came to our class to share about a group within the Catholic Church. They began their presentation with a video of an event where people were dancing, singing, and speaking in tongues. I had never seen anything like this before. They shared that speaking in tongues was in the Bible, in the book of 1 Corinthians 14. They went on to explain that God had gifts He wanted to bless and fill us with the Holy Spirit. They had a name for these believers, it was the Charismatic Movement.

Not being familiar with the Catholic faith, I didn't know if this was happening in all churches or just within the Catholic Church. I came from a church that was pretty conservative. Some of the ladies at my church still wore coverings on their heads as a sign of submission to men. It's not that people didn't have fun or laugh at my church, but joy was not a theme that was preached, from what I could remember. So the nuns' presentation gave me pause for thought on the true nature of God.

There was a panel of men and women that came the following week. They were from a pro-life group making a presentation about what actually happens when a woman has an abortion. I already had my preconceived ideas about this topic and was not sure they would be able to sway my current understanding. Having compassion on a few of my high school classmates who had become pregnant and opted to have an abortion seemed like a clear choice for them to make at that time.

They gave each one of us a trifold pamphlet that had two tiny feet on the front that were very red and were held between a thumb and finger of an adult. They said that the feet of the baby on the brochure was killed at twelve weeks gestation by saline or salt water which was injected into the mother's womb. I was getting uncomfortable. This was not the blob of tissue I was told about. These were two tiny human feet.

They went on to explain that a saline abortion would burn the outer layer of skin and the baby would die. I started to become nauseous, because I had never known what actually happened in an abortion. This seemed so cruel and inhumane. They went on to share two other kinds of abortion. I was not aware that there were various ways to do an abortion, so I braced myself for more of this shocking information.

The second procedure they explained was the Dilatation and Evacuation abortion. This is when the baby is suctioned out of the mother's womb. There is something like a vacuum with a tube attached which was inserted into the uterus to remove the living baby by literally sucking it out through this tube. The remains of the baby coming through this tube went into a large round glass container so the contents could be examined.

Dilatation and Curettage was the third type of abortion procedure that was explained to our class. The doctor would take a sharp tool and insert it into the uterus and begin to cut up the baby's body and remove it from the mother's womb. The doctor would have to take stock of all the parts of the baby to make sure all pieces were accounted for.

They showed us slides on a screen in the front of the class. There were images of the by-products of each type of abortion. Little bodies burned by the saline solution lying there with no life in them, blackened by the salt solution. Fluid with body parts floating about in a glass beaker; a hand here and perfectly formed feet lying separate from the rest of the body. I was in utter shock. If people knew the truth they would never consent to this barbaric practice which was beyond comprehension.

There had been no education on this subject until this day. Sickened and numb from this horrifying information spelled out so clearly with horrid pictures of children's lives that were wiped out. Did the media lie to us that this was just a blob of tissue? Would educating people make the difference? My heart and mind made a one hundred and eighty degree turnaround that day. I was no longer pro-choice, but pro-life!

Their presentation did not end with this information, they said the very reasons used to get abortion legal would be the same problems that would destroy our society. The sanctity of life had now been devalued and would affect all human life. One of the arguments used to get abortion legal was the abuse of women and children.

They said legalized abortion would increase women being beaten and raped. Children's lives would be at risk for they were not seen as a gift from God, but as a burden, and child abuse would increase instead of decrease. What was meant to help women would bring more harm.

This pro-life group brought up more issues of child abuse that I had never heard about. Adults would use children for their own sexual gratification such as incest with family members. They explained that the parameters of right and wrong were being blurred and pedophilia would eventually be accepted as a normal relationship. They went on to say that it would create a slow erosion to the moral fabric of our society. Another by-product of abortion would also be the affect on our economy as fewer people would be born.

To say I was inundated by the revelation of facts that were shared was an understatement. The images and details of how this would affect our society consumed my thoughts. Knowing the stark reality of the measures used to end another person's life changed me. It was not just tissue, but another human being with the potential for a great and purposeful life.

I became the annoying person trying to buttonhole family and friends with the new information that was learned. I was on a mission to educate them on this extremely sensitive issue. I was unable to have the same impact the group had on me and there was no one who really wanted to hear what I had to say.

My zeal may have come across as condescending, but that was not my intention. Somehow, the task of changing the world seemed like an impossibility. Life had taken on a whole new dimension for me. I found out what actually happened when an abortion was done and there was no turning back to the lies I once believed.

Other topics seemed trivial after this. Like an experiment we had to do for our Psychology class. We were instructed to open the door for people and document their reaction, whether they were a male or female. We were set up to do research with graphs, tracking the number of people, and time of day. We had to write a paper on our findings as to peoples' reactions and our personal observations to this information.

It is amazing how many variables affected the outcome of this particular project. We had fun watching people throughout the day. The time of day did factor into the responses we received. Were people hungry or tired? These variables seemed to play into our results.

Things were moving along in other subjects and I was making significant headway on my research paper. We needed to cite ten sources to substantiate the content of our writing. My topic was on happiness and that would seem like a broad topic.

One word that kept coming up in my research was "joy." Joy is a more intense emotion than happiness, more like what those nuns experienced in their charismatic group. Happiness is a contentment of feeling unfettered by problems. A blending of joy and happiness may leave you blissful. However, just because I was researching this topic did not mean I was experiencing it.

In Anatomy and Physiology, we were beginning to learn about the different muscles groups and how they worked. There were three different kinds of muscles. There was the skeletal, smooth, and cardiac muscles. All these are vital to our health and well-being.

It was so interesting to learn all this information while gaining a better understanding of the body and how it works. All the babies that were aborted had all the body systems we do, except they are in the very early stage of formation when a woman would not even know she was pregnant. When you have a purpose for learning, it takes on a greater significance for the need to know that information.

My friend, Lyn, and I would sit in the stairwell of our dorm to talk. We would talk about everything that was relevant to us. School work, boyfriends, what we hoped for in the future, and many other things. She had been going out with her boyfriend for four years and was hoping to get married in the near future and have a lot of children after she graduated. I said I wanted to have a career and maybe have children after I turned thirty.

We often came to this spot over the months to talk about events in our lives. Lyn was really smart and had gotten a very high score on her SAT's. She would often help her boyfriend, who was at another college, with his research papers. I thought he was taking advantage of her for his own personal gain.

After the last paper she wrote for him, he broke up with her and said he had a new girlfriend. She was devastated; she thought she knew her future and all of a sudden that future was gone. She cried and lamented how this had changed everything. My job was to encourage her that a better tomorrow was on the horizon.

It was a Saturday night and the other girls who were spending the weekend on campus had organized a poker game. This was not your regular poker game for cash prizes; there were alcoholic beverages secretly brought in to lighten the mood. We were going to play a game of strip poker and we only had girls in our dorm. Every time you lost a hand, you would lose a piece of your clothing. First the socks, then the jeans, a shirt, bra, underpants and the loser was required to run through the halls of the dorm with no clothes singing "Joy to the World."

After eleven hands I had come out as the designated loser. If it wasn't for the alcohol, this would have been more humiliating than I thought at the time. A quick jog through the upstairs and downstairs hallways singing and I quickly slipped back into my clothes and I was out of the game. That was all right, because I was tired and ready for bed. They continued to play and periodically I would hear someone running by my room singing as they traversed through the hallways.

The next day was Sunday and I got a call from Dean. He called to let me know his old girlfriend had tried to kill herself. Evidently her current boyfriend had two girlfriends. The other girl became pregnant and he had chosen to marry her and have the baby together. Dean was trying to be supportive to his previous girlfriend and talked her out of committing suicide.

I sent a note of encouragement to her and offered whatever help I could. I don't think this was the help she wanted. I later heard she had a fight at school with the pregnant girl and it did not go well. She was deeply hurt by the turn of events that were painful and humiliating.

I know Dean's intentions were meant to help her, but I believe her intentions were to restore the relationship they once had. Being so far away, it was hard to know all the facts and what was happening. I wasn't going to let it bother me because there were so many good things happening and my research from my paper on happiness became more applicable now than ever.

"Life's under no obligation to give us
what we expect."

- Margaret Mitchell

CHAPTER 11
NOVEMBER - THE ELECTION

The elections were November 2nd and we had a new president: Jimmy Carter. He was a peanut farmer and the former governor of the state of Georgia. He won the election against Gerald Ford, who was the incumbent president. All this seemed very confusing as the line of command had changed so many times over the past couple of years.

Dean was able to vote, but I was too young. He said he would not tell me who he voted for because I had not voted. I felt this was unfair because I would have voted if I could have. President Jimmy Carter was the elected thirty-ninth president. The nation was hoping for some normalcy after the turmoil of the last three years.

With my new revelations on abortion, I think that the Roe v. Wade decision slipped through as there were so many other pressing issues. Our country was blindsided by something they didn't know the ramifications of, with all the upheaval in our government at this time. In retrospect, someone had an agenda and they just ran it through until it became law. In our constitution, it says liberty and justice for all. What about the rights of the unborn?

———————————

My mom had appendicitis when she was three months pregnant with me. I'm sure they gave her options, as she needed to have her appendix removed at this time. Thinking about what she went through so I could be born is very humbling. My grandmother told me many times that they were worried that something would be wrong with me. At that time, my mother was given a drug to keep her from miscarrying.

Many years later, she found out that women who took this drug while in the early months of a pregnancy had daughters who were unable to have children. She now had a new worry, would her daughter be able to have children? I was not concerned about this since I was just seventeen and unmarried. Mothers have a heightened level of responsibility for the health and well-being of their children.

Monday was here and there was a little over six weeks left in the semester. I enjoyed my classes and looked forward to each one as new information was taught and learned. We had fun times too, but we were learning to find a balance and become more responsible with our time. We still took the time for those late night chats in the stairwell where we would solve the problems of the world, or at least explore the possibilities of the future. Friendships are important.

The middle of the month was closing in fast. I would be going home for the weekend to attend my brother Stan's wedding. They would be having a small service with family at our church. I enjoyed listening to my mixed tape of America, Kansas, Cat Stevens, and many more musical artists on my long drive home. I did not make any stops other than to fill up my gas tank.

I was listening to the music very loud while traveling along with no cars in sight. I was about halfway home when a car pulled up beside me. It was a State Police Officer in an unmarked car and he motioned for me to pull off to the side of the road. Needless to say, I was shaking. You rely on the pace of cars around you to keep going the proper speed limit.

I was the only one on the highway until he came and pulled me over. He got out of his car and walked up to my window. He asked me, "Do you know how fast you were going?" I told him, "I do not know." He said, "You were going forty miles over the speed limit and will be getting a ticket." He asked for my driver's license and insurance card which I pulled out of the glove box. He went back to his car to write up the ticket.

When he returned, he gave me the ticket, which was over one hundred dollars. He asked me, "Why were you going so fast?"

I said, "I didn't realize I was going that fast because there were no other cars around me at the time." He asked, "Where are you going?", and I told him, "I am heading home from school for my brother's wedding".

He assured me that my safety was his greatest concern and he wanted me to get home alive. Wow, that was an eye opening experience. I said, "thank you" and he returned to his car, but waited for me to pull out first. He followed me for a while to make sure I was traveling at a safe speed. I turned the music down so I could focus on driving safely.

I arrived home late Friday night and the wedding would be at two o'clock the next day. Both families were in attendance, along with our two families pastors. They would officiate the service with Stan and Leann's handwritten vows. The pastors had a sermon on love and family life.

The bride's dress was classically beautiful with long sleeves and a high neckline. She had an empire waistband where the silky fabric flowed down to the floor with a train coming from the back of the dress. She held a cascading bouquet of roses with ivy greens. My brother had bought a lovely, dark-brown suit for the occasion with a little rose boutonnière on his lapel.

I did not buy a special dress for this occasion and wore the dress that had been purchased for my senior pictures. My boyfriend wore a blue blazer with a pair of brown dress pants. My brother and his new wife, Leann, had a catered meal at their home for our families and the pastors.

This would be the first time many of us would be seeing their new home. It was a two-story with the living room, kitchen, laundry, and dining room on the lower floor. The upstairs had three bedrooms and a bathroom. It had a brick front and the rest of the home had a cream colored aluminum siding. It was nice to visit with family and hear what they were doing and the plans they were making.

Congratulations were said and goodbye hugs were given. I had laundry to do and a paper to type up for the following week. I was not fast at typing so it would be a rather long, laborious process. My mom could probably type ninety words a minute; if I would ask her, she would type up my paper from my handwritten copy.

I was trying to show them that I was more ambitious than they thought. I would slowly peck out each word. My laundry needed to be washed before I headed back to school, so I was working on that too. My parents were a little surprised at the initiative I was taking to get things done.

I left early Sunday afternoon to go back to school. I was greeted by Jan who had just returned from a weekend at home. She was so happy and I'm sure her family missed her joyful disposition to brighten their days. Things were going well for her as we both spent our evening preparing for the next day's classes. We didn't have any classes together and we only seemed to connect at the end of the day.

The week went by quickly and we decided to go to an event where a hypnotist was the main act at another local college. We had a difficult time finding a parking space, but there was a small space between two cars that I tried to back into. Well, it didn't take long for us to find out the space was too small as I backed right into one of the cars and put a dent in it. The girls wanted me to just pull out and find another space, but I had to find the owner of the vehicle I had backed into.

I ran into the nearby dorm to see if anyone there knew whose car was parked out front. They directed me down the hall to the fifth door on the right. I knocked on the door and a girl with tousled blond hair answered. I asked her, "Are you the owner of the red car out front?" She said, "I am".

I went on to explain that I had backed into her car and it left a dent. She came out to look at it, but the thing that shocked her the most was the fact that I took the time to find her. I gave her my insurance information and she thanked me profusely. It felt good to do the right thing.

We were able to find a large parking space and get to the theatre in time for the show. The hypnotist chose Father Jones as his volunteer. He had talked Father Jones into believing he was on a boat. The hypnotist asked him what he saw while he was on the boat. Father Jones said he saw a gorgeous woman in a bikini. We laughed so hard, because he was so serious when he said it and was so out of character for him.

"In three words I can sum up everything I've learned about life: it goes on."

- Robert Frost

CHAPTER 12
DECEMBER - LIVING TRUTH

The first weekend in December proved to be a fun time. The school sat on a high mountain and got considerably more snow than the rest of the area that surrounded it. I never saw so much snow in December. My classmates said that there was a toboggan in the basement. So, a group of us went there to retrieve it and make sure it was still in one piece. It looked like it was still in working order, just covered in cobwebs and dust.

There was a very steep and long hill out by the power lines and this would be our destination. After everyone had bundled up in whatever outerwear they had brought to school, we started our trek through the wooded area until we came into the clearing at the power lines. Looking down the steep incline was frightening and to think, we were about to sit on a wooden board and sail down this hill!

My heart sank to my feet and I began having second thoughts. We were hoping to get twelve people onto this large toboggan. The courage of everyone else bolstered my confidence. Everyone was taking their places and they suggested I sit in the very front. There would be no turning back in fear being in this position. We all loaded onto the toboggan while those in the back held on and would take a running jump to hop onto it once we were moving.

Initially we were moving slowly, but it did not take long for this group of thrill seekers to encounter the experience they were looking for. The snow was lightly pelting my face when we first started going down the hill. It wasn't long until my face was completely covered and I was unable to see. Someone was yelling out, "lean to the left!", then, "lean to the right!" Those who could see were helping us maneuver down this steep incline safely. The whole group was bouncing along over the dips and valleys. We were laughing, screaming, and crying all at the same time.

Many of us were not properly dressed for this momentous occasion. The exhilaration of the experience left us warm and out of breath as we reached the bottom of the hill. We were brushing our snow-caked clothes off and trying to get our bearings. Looking up the hill we had just come down was an "oh my goodness" moment. It must have been a quarter-mile long and the thought of taking the toboggan up again was dizzying to think about. We all joined together and made this journey up the hill laughing, and inhaling deeply, as we rose up with each step.

It was hard to believe that we were coming to the end of this semester. So much had happened over the past several months. A surprising turn of events was becoming a pro-life advocate. They had just voted to keep abortions illegal in the Netherlands. Many young women in our country were not being told the truth. Educating the public on this issue with facts would be vital in saving lives.

My fever for being pro-life had not diminished, I just didn't know what to do with the information I had learned. Even though we were at a Catholic college, not all my classmates were pro-life and believed that abortion was a valid form of birth control. They said they were not ready for that responsibility. Many would strongly consider it if they found themselves pregnant and unmarried as a viable option.

The Snowflake Ball was coming up and would mark the end of the semester. I thought it would be a great opportunity to wear the dress I had bought for the prom. I called Dean to see if he wanted to go to the dance with me. He said, "I'll come if we can spend the night at a hotel." I said, "I will not." I thought that was the end of that.

The weekend of the dance Lyn came running down the hall and said someone was here to see me. The only people who had come to visit me at school were my parents and my friend Kate. I quickly ran down the hall with her into the foyer and there was

Dean. He had come to take me to the dance. Little did he know my dress and shoes were still at my parents home.

I was a little dumbfounded and unsure what to do at this point. Lyn was all giddy, standing there waiting to be introduced. So, I introduced her to Dean and they had a cordial conversation. I honestly was at a loss for words. He suggested we find a nice restaurant, but I never ate out up here so I had no clue where to go. He thought we could wing it and find something nearby.

We found a small, out-of-the-way restaurant. The food was good, but I was still surprised and did not have much of an appetite. Dean said he was getting a room at a local motel and suggested we go there to watch TV. I was a little skeptical, but I thought, what are we going to do anyway. For some reason, when we got to the room and turned on the television, Sesame Street was on and we decided to watch this children's show.

It was getting late and some of my classmates were coming to the hotel with their dates. Not that this made it right, but others were spending the night here too. I thought, "one night, what can it hurt?" Back at the school, Lyn realized I was not going to be back before the curfew. She signed me out so I would not get in trouble.

I thanked Lyn for signing me out so I wouldn't have any repercussions. Our last few days of classes were upon us. We would all be heading home for the Christmas break. I think my classes went well, but these last few days would determine the final outcome. We would have our final grades sent to us after we got home.

Everybody was leaving at different times due to class schedules. Jan started packing Wednesday morning because she was being picked up at lunchtime. We said our farewells in the morning. Lyn and myself were packing up later in the afternoon after our last class. Her mother was picking her up and I would miss our late night stairwell conversations. I put all my stuff in my car and was headed for home too.

Christmas was right around the corner and everyone was getting ready by decorating and buying gifts. My Dad came home with a tree that we would decorate while we listened to a

Christmas album on the stereo. My favorite part of trimming the tree was putting the tinsel on the branches as symmetrically as possible on each branch.

One tradition over the Holiday season was to watch the Charlie Brown Christmas, a timeless classic. The Bing Crosby White Christmas special had festive music and my Dad's favorite comedic actor Jackie Gleason played the part of Santa Claus. There was one more seasonal favorite, "It's a Wonderful Life", with James Stewart. This movie helped you reevaluate what and who was truly important in life.

My Mom would be baking some of our favorite cookies like date nut pinwheels, sand tarts, peanut butter, and her delicious fruitcakes too. She would make her filling ahead of time and freeze it. She said it had a better flavor after being frozen and then would bake it on Christmas Day.

Oyster filling was made the day of the meal with fresh oysters. A Waldorf salad was a new addition to the regular menu. My Grandmother brought the mince pie that some would put a little whiskey on before they ate it. These were just a few of the dishes we could look forward to.

Mom was preparing to entertain over twenty family members at this holiday meal. My Grandmother, Grandfather, Great Aunt Millie, Uncle John, cousins, and more were there to celebrate with us. With all the people in our house it was really noisy and hot. Christmas day brought some surprises as Dean gave me an oil painting set with several canvases as a Christmas present.

The holidays were over and I found myself extremely tired. I was sleeping all night and taking naps in the day. My mom was concerned that I might have the flu and wanted me to go to the doctor. I thought I was tired from all the ruckus at the house over the holidays.

A letter came in the mail from my college. I assumed it was my grades and it was. My grade point average was higher than anticipated. My Mom was surprised and shared something with me that my first grade teacher had said to her, that I would never be better than an average student.

My Dad was quiet and somehow I think he never believed what that teacher had said so many years ago. He was always encouraging me to study more and work harder. He looked at the grades as if he knew I was capable of doing well. They were both glad that their youngest child was growing up and assuming more responsibility.

My college classes were already chosen for the Spring semester and would continue with my current program. I was missing my new friends, but I would be going to Karen's house for a New Years Eve Party. I hadn't seen her since the Summertime.

Dean had made plans with a friend of his to go out on New Years Eve. We had gotten together earlier that day and I told him that I had been really tired. He asked me, "Do you think you are pregnant?" I said, "I don't know." He encouraged me that we would take it one day at a time.

We went our separate ways that evening to bring in the new year. The future was put aside for now to have fun with our friends.

"The most important thing is to enjoy your life, to be happy, it's all that matters."
- Audrey Hepburn

Conclusion:
JANUARY - NEXT FEW YEARS

I returned to college the middle of January. I felt like I had the flu and was nauseous and felt very tired all the time. My roommate was concerned and suggested I go see a doctor. Friends were stopping by because they heard I wasn't feeling well and I would be sleeping most of the time.

Well it was inevitable, I looked in the local yellow pages for a doctor and made an appointment. The day of the doctor appointment arrived and none too soon for my roommate, coming from a family of doctors and nurses she knew something was wrong.

The doctor greeted me and introduced himself and shook my hand. He asked me what the problem seemed to be. I said I was nauseous and very tired. He said he wanted to do a test of my urine and blood. He said after they got the results we would meet in his office.

He called me back to his office and cleared his throat, he said, "I have the results to your tests and I know why you have not been feeling well and are tired." The doctor looked me straight in the eye with great compassion and said, "You are pregnant."

He added that there were only two options for someone in my circumstances, he said, "You could marry the father and raise the child together or you could put the baby up for adoption." I started to cry and he came around the desk to give me a fatherly hug of comfort.

He said, "You have a big decision ahead of you, but I would take time to talk to the father of the child and make your choice from there. Again those are your only two choices." I could not appreciate his kindness and compassion at the time. I honestly believe God directed me to this doctor.

My roommate asked if the visit with the doctor went well. I said it did, but did not offer any particulars. I asked my one friend who spent the weekends at school with me if we could meet later and we scheduled a meeting in the stairwell at the end of the day.

After supper I called my boyfriend and told him the news the doctor had given me. He was thrilled at the prospect of being a dad. He said if I came home this weekend he would talk to my parents for me and ask my parents permission to marry me. He was shouldering the responsibility for our actions and it gave me courage to move forward.

I met my friend at the stairwell to talk that evening. She said there were other ways of handling this situation. I didn't respond, but the other ways she was referencing was not an option.

The weekend was here and the trip home seemed to take forever. When I got home my mom had already figured out why I had come home this weekend. I had never considered the shame and embarrassment this would cause my parents.

Dean said he would come over that evening to talk to my parents. When he came over my Dad was asleep on the sofa. My mom, Dean, and I were sitting on the edge of our seats waiting for him to wake up. A short evening nap was part of his routine.

All in the Family was the show that was on the television at that time. My Dad woke up and Dean greeted him. He went on to ask my Dad for my hand in marriage and explained that I was pregnant and we were going to have a baby.

To say the least, the revelation took him by surprise and he gave his verbal acknowledgement that he understood and thanked Dean for coming to tell him. One question he had for me was, "Are you going to be finishing school?" I had briefly thought about this and determined you could not focus on starting a family while going to school.

I went to talk to the dean, after returning from weekend, and told her I would be leaving college. She asked why and I told her I was pregnant. She was gracious and wished me well in the future. I packed up my things while everyone was at class. I could not face my roommate and tell her the truth.

We got married in March of 1977 and our baby boy was born in September of that year. My Mother and Grandmother were there to greet him after he was born. The realization that you are responsible for the moral upbringing of another person is overwhelming.

I was on a journey to know God and live life by His principles found in the Bible. He is an ever-present help in times of trouble. God's love supersedes all our mistakes and it says He wants to lead us on paths of righteousness for His names sake. It was humbling that the pro-life group came to share the truth. So many believe the lie and are suffering the consequences of bad decisions they have made.

Years later as a wife and mother with three small children, I was in search of the Holy Spirit that those happy nuns shared with us years ago. I went with my children to a Bible study down the street in an old farmhouse. The pastor and his wife greeted us as we came to the door. A group of musicians played some beautiful songs, we sang along in praise, and worship.

The pastor had a deep teaching that he shared from the word of God. Everyone was attentive to the scriptures he shared with us. After the teaching, he began to pray for people. I asked to be baptized in the Holy Spirit and the pastor prayed for me and I received the gift of tongues and prayed through the night. Many of the prayers were miraculously answered.

John 3:16 For God so loved the world, that he gave his only begotten Son, that whosoever believeth in him should not perish, but have everlasting life.

Romans 8:26 Likewise the Spirit also helpeth our infirmities: for we know not what we should pray for as we ought: but the Spirit itself maketh intercession for us with groanings which cannot be uttered.

Romans 15:13 Now the God of hope fill you with all joy and peace in believing, that ye may abound in hope, through the power of the Holy Ghost.

Prayer for Salvation -

Dear Lord Jesus, Come into my heart.

Forgive me of my sin. Wash me and cleanse me.

Set me free, Jesus.

Thank You that You died for me.

I believe that You are risen from the dead

and that You're coming back again for me.

Fill me with the Holy Spirit.

Give me a passion for the lost,

a hunger for the things of God

and a holy boldness to preach the

gospel of Jesus Christ.

I'm saved; I'm born again,

I'm forgiven and I'm on my way to

Heaven because I have Jesus in my heart.

Zephaniah 3:17

The Lord thy God in the midst of thee is mighty; he will save, he will rejoice over thee with joy; he will rest in his love, he will joy over thee with singing.

Scriptures are taken from the King James Version of the Bible.

http://www.phmc.state.pa.us/portal/communities/
governors/1951-2015/milton-shapp.html

A History of US by Joy Hakim, From Colonies to Country, 3
A History of the US by Joy Hakim, All the People, 10
Published by Oxford Universty Press, Inc
Copyright © 1993 by Joy Hakim

Made in the USA
Middletown, DE
20 October 2022